"*Ricardo's Theory of Growth and Accumulation* is precise yet attractive to read. Salvadori starts with closed economy analysis, before turning to the open economy and its dynamics. Detailed attention is given to rent theory. Essential reading for Ricardo scholars."

– Ian Steedman, Emeritus Professor of Economics
at Manchester Metropolitan University, UK

T0384092

Ricardo's Theory of Growth and Accumulation

In the aftermath of the Napoleonic Wars Britain found itself faced with a stagnant economy. Economist David Ricardo believed that the full re-integration of Britain into the world market would allow for both capital accumulation and population growth, and used arguments that anticipate ideas entertained in modern contributions to the theory of economic growth and development. However, several of these arguments have not yet been translated into the language of modern classical economics. *Ricardo's Theory of Growth and Accumulation* seeks to overcome this striking lacuna.

The latest entry in the Graz Schumpeter lecture series, this text explores and elaborates Ricardo's arguments and the models utilized by those who subsequently followed in support of his work. The Ricardian system is first examined through a one-sector economy, following Kaldor's model, and a two-sector economy, following Pasinetti's model. These building blocks are developed through the exploration of a small open economy, which allows an analysis of the impact of international trade in exceedingly simple circumstances. This discussion expands further by considering the world economy. More sophisticated variants of the two-sector model are presented, in which commodity prices are endogenously determined by the trading interplay amongst several countries. A final analysis makes Ricardo's case by introducing accumulation in the world economy.

This book is of interest to students and scholars of Ricardo, classical economics, and – more broadly – growth theory, the theory of international economics, and globalization. The author was keen to render the analytical parts compelling to the historian and the historical parts compelling to the theorist.

Neri Salvadori is Professor of Economics at the University of Pisa, Italy.

The Graz Schumpeter Lectures
Series Editor: Richard Sturn, University of Graz, Austria

For more information about this series, please visit: www.routledge.com/The-Graz-Schumpeter-Lectures/book-series/SE0392
    For more information, please visit the Graz Schumpeter Society's website: http://www.uni-graz.at/gsg

Ricardo's Theory of Growth and Accumulation

A Modern View

Neri Salvadori

Routledge
Taylor & Francis Group

LONDON AND NEW YORK

First published 2021
by Routledge
2 Park Square, Milton Park, Abingdon, Oxon OX14 4RN

and by Routledge
605 Third Avenue, New York, NY 10017

First issued in paperback 2022

Routledge is an imprint of the Taylor & Francis Group, an informa business

Publisher's Note
The publisher has gone to great lengths to ensure the quality of this
reprint but points out that some imperfections in the original copies
may be apparent.

British Library Cataloguing-in-Publication Data
A catalogue record for this book is available from the British Library

Library of Congress Cataloging-in-Publication Data
Names: Salvadori, Neri, author.
Title: Ricardo's theory of growth and accumulation:
a modern view / Neri Salvadori.
Description: Abingdon, Oxon; New York, NY: Routledge, 2020. |
Series: The Graz Schumpeter lectures |
Includes bibliographical references and index.
Identifiers: LCCN 2020008470 (print) | LCCN 2020008471 (ebook)
Subjects: LCSH: Ricardo, David, 1772-1823. |
Economic development. | Classical school of economics. | Economics.
Classification: LCC HB103.R5 S23 2020 (print) |
LCC HB103.R5 (ebook) | DDC 330.15/3—dc23
LC record available at https://lccn.loc.gov/2020008470
LC ebook record available at https://lccn.loc.gov/2020008471

ISBN: 978-0-367-50590-5 (pbk)
ISBN: 978-0-367-44410-5 (hbk)
ISBN: 978-1-003-00951-1 (ebk)

DOI: 10.4324/9781003009511

Typeset in Times New Roman
by codeMantra

Contents

Illustrations

Tables

Figures

Preface

It was a great honour to have been invited to give the 2015 Graz Schumpeter Lectures. I was particularly delighted for two reasons. First, this gave me the chance to follow in one of my mentors' footsteps, Ian Steedman, who gave the 1999 Graz Schumpeter Lectures. Second, I received the invitation from a life-long friend and co-author of several papers and books, Heinz D. Kurz, who, I felt, expressed the trust he had in my capabilities: a co-author knows your capabilities and your deficiencies better than anyone else!

I was very concerned with the promise to put my lectures into the form of a book. Today, it has become a habit that scholars write almost exclusively journal articles. Nevertheless, a book is an excellent opportunity for a scholar who has already published several contributions on an issue to bring together and reorganize his (or her) ideas, to present them in a more general framework, to provide readers with more detailed proofs, and to illustrate the argument in terms of numerical examples. Journal articles do not typically provide a platform for an exhaustive treatment of the issues under consideration and do not allow for deeper analyses of specific points. Put briefly, a book based on lectures provides the best format I can think of for a complete and coherent treatment of a subject matter. Since throughout my entire academic career I have repeatedly dealt with various aspects of David Ricardo's contributions to the theory of capital accumulation and economic growth, a suitable subject matter was already close at hand for my 2015 Graz Schumpeter Lectures.

From 1992 onwards Heinz and I had been concerned with this theme, first in a review article of Michio Morishima's book on Ricardo. Subsequently, from 1998 Heinz and I were involved for several years in an analysis of endogenous growth theory which prompted us to stress the fact that this theory was more closely connected to Classical analysis than to Neo-Classical analysis. The cornerstone of our argument was a comparison with Ricardo's theory of growth and accumulation. In 2008, Simone D'Alessandro and I even produced a paper comparing Pasinetti's Ricardian model with an endogenous growth model by Rebelo and its title included the question "Two different models or just one?" More recently, Rodolfo Signorino and I started to analyse the Ricardo-Malthus debate on international trade theory and policy in a number of papers, from both historical and analytical perspectives; this analysis led us to generalize the original Kaldor and Pasinetti Ricardian model to include international trade. Recently, Giuseppe Freni joined us in some of these contributions. These ideas I intended to bring together, develop, and reorganize in my lectures and then in this book.

Readers are now provided with an idea of what they will find in this book, but it is appropriate to specify also what they will *not* find. First of all, I do not deal with technical change. Indeed, the fourth lecture I delivered was on technical change. But when I started to write the book, I discovered that what I had presented in that lecture was not sufficiently integrated with the rest of the undertaking. The five chapters I am presenting constitute a sort of small treatise, moving from the simpler to more difficult aspects, and in some sense it is complete. The content of my fourth lecture in 2015 was *not* a development of the models here presented to take account of technical change; it was an analysis of the famous Chapter XXXI of the *Principles*. (The interested reader can find it in EJHET 2019 as Freni and Salvadori (2019).) The inclusion of this material in the present book would have transformed it into an anthological work on Ricardian issues, and I had no wish to do this. The fact that technical change is not included means that the book deals with what Ricardo called the 'natural' course of the economy: an economic system in which capital accumulates, the population grows, but technical progress is set aside. Hence, the argument is based on the assumption that the set of production processes from which cost-minimizing producers can choose is given and constant. Technical change is, of course, taken to counteract some of the tendencies discussed in this book. The fact that I shall not deal with technical change must, however, not be interpreted that Ricardo did not either or that he was a technological pessimist. The 'natural' course the economy takes expresses counterfactual reasoning on his part and must not be identified with the actual course the economy takes.

The reader will not find a theory of trade of modern industrialized economy. This is mainly a book on Ricardo, and therefore, many of the complexities of the present-day economy are just ignored. However, the fact that the accumulation of capital and the growth of population (with no reference to development and technical change) may take a country from being specialized in an industrial commodity to being specialized in an agricultural commodity could be of some interest even for analysis of the economy in our day and age.

Another issue that is not dealt with is money. Ricardo started (and concluded) his intellectual journey as a monetary economist. Yet I have to confess that I was never much attracted by monetary issues. So I felt unable to deal with money in this book. The interested reader may consult other sources, and among them, I strongly recommend Ghislain Deleplace's *Ricardo on Money: A Reappraisal*.

Let me conclude this introduction with acknowledgements. First of all, I would like to thank my co-authors, mentioned here in alphabetical order: Simone D'Alessandro, Giuseppe Freni, Heinz D. Kurz, and Rodolfo Signorino. Not only did they give me permission to use freely the material that we produced jointly, but they also read and commented on the various chapters of this book while I was drafting them. I have greatly benefited from their suggestions. Other scholars also read and commented on parts of this book, and I want to thank them too: Enrico Bellino, Giacomo Costa, Pompeo Della Posta, Christian Gehrke, Gary Mongiovi, Arrigo Opocher, Susumu Takenaga, Yoshinori Shiozawa, and Ian Steedman.

I warmly thank the Graz Schumpeter Society that invited me to deliver the lectures. I was invited also by the Posgrado de la Facultad de Economia of the UNAM (August 2014 and January 2015) and by Meiji University (September and October 2017) to deliver lectures, and I used much of the material here presented. I want to thank not only the institutions but also the people who attended my lectures and the colleagues who made my stays in Graz, Mexico City, and Tokyo not only intellectually stimulating, but also enjoyable and pleasurable.

My final thought goes to my parents, Angela e Luigi, and to my wife, Rosa Lucia. I owe my parents, who recently passed away, the ability to appreciate the enjoyment that scientific activity alone can give. It is highly doubtful that I could have accomplished whatever I did over the last 30 years without my wife, to whom I am indebted for both her loving attention and her innate ability to create a care-free pleasing environment.

1 The one-sector model

The Works and Correspondence of David Ricardo (hereafter *Works*) had a major impact on the way in which the Classical economists and especially Ricardo were seen. Piero Sraffa's Introduction in Volume I (Sraffa, 1951) "penetrated a hundred years of misunderstanding and distortion" (Eatwell, 1984 [1995], p. 76). In the first half of the twentieth century, following the lead of Alfred Marshall's *Principles of Economics* (1890), a fairly wide consensus dominated the interpretation of the Classical economists' contribution to political economy. In a nutshell, Marshall portrayed Adam Smith, David Ricardo, and other authors he dubbed "Classical" as precursors of his own theory of demand and supply (see, in particular, the famous Appendix I, "Ricardo's theory of value"). By contrast, Sraffa created "a vivid rationale for the structure and content of surplus theory" (Eatwell, *ibidem*). According to Sraffa's interpretation, Classical economists are advocates of a totally different theory, based on what has subsequently been called the "surplus" approach to the theory of value and distribution (see Garegnani, 1984).

Indicative of the attention Sraffa's edition received in those years, let us recall the observations by George J. Stigler in his review of *Works* for the *American Economic Review*:

> Ricardo was a fortunate man. He lived in a period – then drawing to a close – when an untutored genius could still remake economic science. He lived in a nation where two great problems, inflation and free trade, gave direction and significance to economics. And now, 130 years after his death, he is as fortunate as ever: he has been befriended by Sraffa – who has been befriended by Dobb.
>
> (Stigler, 1953, p. 586)

Following Sraffa's interpretation, Ricardo's procedure to tackle the issue of value and distribution (and not that of *capital accumulation* and *growth of population*) may be divided into four steps. The *first* step consisted in eliminating the problem of rent: "By getting rid of rent, which we may do on the corn produced with the capital last employed, and on all commodities produced by labour in manufactures, the distribution between capitalist and labourer becomes a much more simple consideration" (*Works* VIII, p. 194). The *second* step consisted in trying to overcome the problem of value by assuming the "corn model", namely, by assuming the existence of a sector, corn, in which inputs and outputs coincide and, therefore, the rate of profits can be ascertained directly as a ratio of quantities of corn without any need for recourse to prices. Since Ricardo accepted Malthus's criticism that there is no sector in which the commodity produced is exactly of the same kind as the capital advanced, a third step was required. In *On the Principles of Political Economy and Taxation*, Ricardo presented a fully fledged theory of value, according to which the relative value of the various commodities is governed by the quantities of total labour needed for their production. Hence, as Sraffa concluded,

> the rate of profits was no longer determined by the ratio of the corn produced to the corn used up in production, but, instead, by the ratio of the total labour of the country to the labour required to produce the necessaries of that labour.
>
> (1951, p. xxxii)

However, Ricardo soon realized that the labour theory of value cannot be sustained in general. According to Sraffa, the *final* step of Ricardo's efforts to simplify the theory of value and distribution was the search for an "invariable measure of value". It goes without saying that contemporary economists know the mathematical tools required to develop a formally consistent multi-sector analysis and may therefore dispense with simplifications of this kind.

In the propitious climate generated by the publication of *Works*, Kaldor (1955–56, p. 85) developed what has been considered, ever since, the one-sector model of the Ricardian system *par excellence*. Nevertheless, Kaldor justified his exclusive focus on the agricultural sector by claiming that, unlike the industrial sector, in agriculture "both the input (the wage outlay) and the output consist of the same commodity, 'corn'" (p. 86). Therefore, the agricultural rate of profits can be determined straightforwardly as a ratio of physical quantities without the valuation problem that inevitably arises in the industrial sector. As a consequence, if universal free competition obtains and no entry/exit barriers exist, the industrial rate of profits cannot diverge from the agricultural rate of profits in the long run. This clearly echoes the 'corn-model' interpretation of Ricardo's early theory of profits advanced by Sraffa in his Introduction to *Works* (Sraffa, 1951, p. xxxi), an interpretation which Kaldor summarized in a footnote (see Kaldor (1955–56, p. 86, fn 2).[1] Kaldor's acquaintance with Ricardo's economics owes much to Sraffa, who gave Kaldor access to his findings on Ricardo long before 1951. Kaldor recalled the following biographical episode (Marcuzzo, 1986, pp. 49–50). At the beginning of the Second World War, when the London School of Economics was evacuated to Cambridge, Pigou organized a series of lectures on great economists of the past and, as was only natural, asked Sraffa to lecture on Ricardo. The day before the lecture, Sraffa, who suffered from stage fright, asked Kaldor to give the lecture in his place. Kaldor recalls that, on that occasion, he spent three hours in Sraffa's room listening to him speaking about his editorial work on Ricardo, reading Sraffa's own notes, and taking so many notes himself that he could have taught "a beautiful complete course on Ricardo and not just one lecture" (my translation).

Shortly after Kaldor (1955–56), reflecting the same intellectual climate, Paul A. Samuelson (1959a, 1959b) published a contribution in two parts on Ricardo. And two decades later he published a paper on what he called "the canonical classical model of political economy" (Samuelson, 1978). These contributions played an important role in understanding and interpreting Ricardo. To be clear, the "canonical model" is a one-sector model, very similar to the model used by Kaldor (1955–56) and presented in the next section of this chapter. Some of Samuelson's constructions using linear programming (Samuelson, 1959a) are among the antecedents of the construction presented in Section 1.2.

In this chapter, I will present the one-sector model of the Ricardian system. Hence, I assume that only one commodity, corn, exists. Even though I refer to this model as the Kaldor model, it does not faithfully reflect Kaldor's statement since, as mentioned above, he considered the corn sector as one of potentially many sectors present in the economy under scrutiny. The chapter deals, as does the whole book, with what Ricardo called the "natural" course of the economy: an economic system in which capital accumulates, the population grows, but technical progress is set aside. This is based on the assumption that the set of production processes from which cost-minimizing producers can choose is given and constant. These processes are invariant with respect to the scale of production, but diminishing returns prevail in agriculture since the existing amounts of the different qualities of land are given and finite. The model itself is presented in Section 1.1; Sections 1.2–1.4 are devoted to analysing some of the assumptions adopted in Section 1.1; Section 1.5 shows that Ricardo treated capital accumulation and population growth as endogenous; Section 1.6 compares Ricardo's model with contemporary endogenous growth models, developed in the second part of the 1980s; Section 1.7 concludes the chapter.

1.1 The model[2]

Let us consider an economy in which there are three social classes and just one commodity. The social classes are workers, capitalists, and landlords. Workers provide labour power; they live on their wages and have no other source of income. Capitalists make investments by advancing wages to workers and obtain profits on their investments; they neither work nor own land. Landlords own land and live by renting it out to capitalists. The only commodity produced is corn; it is an agricultural commodity, produced by means of labour and a natural resource, land, which cannot be produced and is assumed to be indestructible. As regards income expenditure, Say's Law holds and, accordingly, all incomes are spent. Workers, landowners, and capitalists are assumed to spend their income on corn.[3] Universal free competition obtains.

Presentation can be made by means of a simple diagram, Figure 1.1, which is an amended version of Kaldor's original diagram: along the vertical axis are units of corn and along the horizontal axis are units of labour. The marginal product curve *MP* is supposed to be continuous.

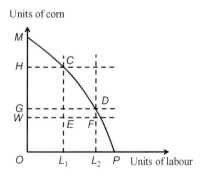

Figure 1.1 The *MP* curve.

Total output at a given amount of labour can be ascertained as the area under the *MP* curve in the interval from zero to that amount of labour. The role of 'capital' in this model may appear puzzling. From a purely technological point of view, there is no technical capital proper in the model. However, capitalists obtain their profits since production requires time and wages need to be advanced to workers at the beginning of the production cycle. For this reason labour is quite commonly referred to as labour-cum-capital, but I will refrain from this use. Because of diminishing returns in agriculture,[4] curve *MP* falls as more units of labour are applied to the existing amounts of the different qualities of land. Given the classical assumption of a constant real wage rate (the 'natural rate of wages'), the rate of wages is *OW* and when OL_1 units of labour are employed, the total wages bill, which coincides with total capital, is given by the area of the rectangle $OWEL_1$. As is well known, differential rent theory allowed Ricardo to tackle the problem of determining prices, profits, and wages by focusing on marginal, i.e. non-rent, land, as Ricardo made clear in a letter to McCulloch, dated 13 June 1820, and quoted above, *Works* VIII, p. 194.

Hence for each unit of labour employed, rent equals the difference between the product of that unit of labour and the product of the unit of labour employed less productively. As a consequence, total rent equals the surface below the *MP* curve and above the segment *HC*. Total profits are a 'residuum', i.e. what remains of corn output after the payment of total rents and the wages bill, and are given by the area of the rectangle *HWEC*. The rate of profits is the ratio of profits over capital, which coincides with the wages bill. Hence, the rate of profits is the ratio of the areas of two rectangles which have the same width. Hence, the ratio of the two areas equals the ratio of the two heights: *WH/OW*.

As capital accumulates and the working population grows, the wages bill increases (proportionally since the real wage is assumed to be constant) and rent payments increase (more than proportionally because of diminishing returns). Overall profits may increase or decrease, but the rate of profits decreases. As we have seen, the rate of profits is the ratio of the areas of two rectangles which have the same width, and whereas the height in the denominator is constant (the wage rate), the height in the numerator decreases as further units of labour are applied to the given plots of land. The pace of capital accumulation decreases since Ricardo assumed that it positively depends on the rate of profits: as the latter declines, the former follows suit. Capital accumulation ceases when employment is OL_2, and the rate of profits has fallen to *DF/OW*, which is the minimum rate of profits necessary in order to induce capital accumulation. In Ricardo's own words:

> The farmer and manufacturer can no more live without profit, than the labourer without wages. Their motive for accumulation will diminish with every diminution of profit, and will cease altogether when their profits are so low as not to afford them an adequate compensation for their trouble, and the risk which they must necessarily encounter in employing their capital productively.
>
> (*Works* I, p. 122)

In the resulting Ricardian 'stationary state', rents equal the area below the MP curve and above the segment GD, profits equal the area of the rectangle $WGDF$, and wages equal the area of the rectangle $OWFL_2$.

On the assumption of a given and constant real wage rate and on the assumption that corn cannot be produced without land, the rate of profits is bound to fall: due to extensive and intensive diminishing returns on land, "with every increased portion of capital employed on it, there will be a decreased rate of production" (*Works* I, p. 98). Diminishing returns thus involve decreasing profitability. If the only source of savings is profits, a falling rate of profits involves a falling rate of capital accumulation. Hence, the dynamics of the economy under scrutiny depends closely on the dynamics of profits. On these assumptions, Ricardo's 'natural' course will end up in a stationary state (apart from very special cases, discussed in Section 1.5). This is so because technical progress has been put on one side. Otherwise technical progress could offset the impact of the 'niggardliness of nature' on the rate of profit.

1.2 On the MP curve[5]

The Kaldor model described above rests on the MP curve. In this section, I clarify what it is and how it is built. This will clarify what is to be meant by diminishing returns. In order to accomplish this task, I use a technology with a finite number of processes, with the proviso that when the number of processes goes to infinity, the MP curve may well become a smooth curve, like that used in Figure 1.1.

Let us consider an economy in which a commodity, corn, is produced by means of land and labour. Following Ricardo, who refers to "the original and indestructible powers of the soil" (*Works* I, p. 67), the available land is in a cultivable state and its cultivation does not alter the quality of the land. Several different *qualities of land* (for short *lands*) exist, and their amounts are taken to be given and finite. Several processes of production are available for each land. Labour is of uniform quality, and workers' skills are conceived as naturally given (there is no human capital accumulation). *Cost-minimizing* behaviour on the part of producers is assumed. For the sake of simplicity, the possibility that agents may try to limit competition or strategically take advantage of special conditions is ignored. In particular, it is supposed that land owners do not collude and do not act as a single monopolist on their resource or take advantage of the distribution of plots of land in order to get an extra-rent; for this reason, the distribution of plots of land among land owners is ignored.[6] Land has no use other than being employed in corn production; consequently, the *reservation price* of the use of land is zero and no land can yield its proprietor a positive rent unless that land is scarce, that is, unless it is in short supply with respect to the amount of corn to be produced. Unlike land which is indestructible and suffers no wear and tear when used, the working life of a given human being is finite and the economy's overall population of workers must be constantly (re)produced. Accordingly, the long-run reservation price of labour reflects a subsistence level, which is taken as given at level $\bar{x}$.

Production is a time-consuming process; the length of the production period is assumed to be uniform across all different lands and all alternative processes of production available to cultivate them; we shall call this period of production a "year": at the beginning of the year labourers cultivate the land and at its end they harvest the crop. Wages are paid at the beginning of the year (or *ante factum*), whereas rents are paid at the end of the year (or *post factum*). The assumption of a *post-factum* payment of rent is necessary in order to make wages the only "capital" advanced at the beginning of the production period by capitalists. Accordingly, profits are calculated only on advanced wages and not on advanced wages and rent (see the previous section). There is no commodity input in production apart from corn as a means of subsistence for the workers. The "wage-plus-profit-per-unit-of-labour" $w = \bar{x}(1 + r)$ is also referred to as the *post-factum* wage rate. By contrast, $\bar{x}$ is the *ante factum* wage rate corresponding to the real wage rate and hence to segment OW in Figure 1.1 of the previous section.[7]

The technology can be represented as a set of processes; returns to scale with regard to each process are constant. Hence, each process can be described as follows:

t acres of land $i \oplus l$ hours of labour $\rightarrow$ 1 bushel of corn.   (1)

The symbol "$\rightarrow$" stands for the "black box" in which labourers working for l hours at a given intensity of work on t acres of land i generate 1 bushel of corn during a yearly production cycle. The symbol "$\oplus$"

indicates that both inputs, i.e. land i and labour, are required in definite proportions to produce corn. For the sake of simplicity, we also write

$$t_{ij} \oplus l_{ij} \to 1$$

where i refers to the quality of land and j to the process employed. Hence, a process is well defined by an amount of land of a given quality and an amount of labour, i.e. it may be indicated by the pair $\left(t_{ij}, l_{ij}\right)$. We will exclude all dominated processes. A process is dominated if it uses more inputs than a convex combination of other processes. The existing m_i (non-dominated) processes using land i can be numbered in such a way that

$$l_{i1} < l_{i2} < \ldots < l_{im_i} \tag{2}$$

Indeed if $l_{ij} = l_{ij+1}$, then at least one of the two processes $\left(t_{ij}, l_{ij}\right)$ and $\left(t_{ij+1}, l_{ij+1}\right)$ is dominated. For the same reason,

$$t_{i1} > t_{i2} > \ldots > t_{im_i} \tag{3}$$

Indeed if $t_{ij} \leq t_{ij+1,}$, then process $\left(t_{ij+1}, l_{j+1}\right)$ is dominated by process $\left(t_{ij}, l_j\right)$. Obviously, the existing n lands can be numbered in such a way that

$$l_{11} \leq l_{21} \leq \ldots \leq l_{n1} \tag{4}$$

Accordingly, the cheapest process when land is not scarce is process (t_{11}, l_{11}).

If the process $\left(t_{ij}, l_{ij}\right)$ is operated, then

$$t_{ij} q_i + w l_{ij} = 1 \tag{5}$$

where $q_i \geq 0$ is the rent per acre (or rate of rent) of land i and $w \geq \bar{x}$ is the *post-factum* wage rate. Moreover, in a long-period position no process can yield a surplus; otherwise all farmer-capitalists would prefer to operate the surplus-yielding process. Therefore in a long-period position,

$$t_{ij} q_i + w l_{ij} \geq 1 \tag{6}$$

for each process $\left(t_{ij}, l_{ij}\right)$, whether or not it is operated. Obviously whether or not a process is operated depends on the amount of corn produced G and the existing amounts of the n lands that are given at levels $T_1, T_2, \ldots, T_n$, respectively. When land i is cultivated but not fully cultivated, we say that land i is *marginal*.

Let us use G as a parameter. It is possible to prove the following propositions. Proofs are in the Mathematical Appendix to this chapter.

Proposition 1. If in a long-period position land i is marginal, then necessarily $q_i = 0$, only the process (t_{i1}, l_{i1}) is operated on land i,

$$w = \frac{1}{l_{i1}} \tag{7}$$

$$G_{-i} \leq G \leq G_{-i} + \frac{T_i}{t_{i1}} \tag{8}$$

where G_{-i} is the amount of corn produced on all lands but land i.

Proposition 2. If in a long-period position land i is fully cultivated and the two non-dominated processes (t_{ij}, l_{ij}) and (t_{ij+h}, l_{ij+h}) are operated, then $h = 1$,

$$w = \frac{t_{ij} - t_{ij+1}}{l_{ij+1}t_{ij} - l_{ij}t_{ij+1}} \tag{9}$$

$$G_{-i} + \frac{T_i}{t_{ij}} \leq G \leq G_{-i} + \frac{T_i}{t_{ij+1}} \tag{10}$$

Proposition 3. If in a long-period position land i is fully cultivated and only process (t_{ij}, l_{ij}) is operated, then

$$G = G_{-i} + \frac{T_i}{t_{ij}}$$

Proposition 4. If in a long-period position s lands are cultivated, then the cultivated lands are lands $1, 2, \ldots, s$.

Proposition 5.[8] If in a long-period position lands $1, 2, \ldots, s$ are cultivated and the others are not, then either

(a) $q_s = 0$ and $G_{-s} \leq G \leq G_{-s} + T_s/t_{s1}$ or

(b) processes (t_{ij}, l_j) and (t_{ij+1}, l_{ij+1}) are operated for some $i \leq s$ and some $j \leq m_i - 1$ and $G_{-i} + T_i/t_{ij} \leq G \leq G_{-i} + T_i/t_{ij+1}$ or

(c) lands $1, 2, \ldots, s$ are fully cultivated, only s processes are operated, call them (t_{1j_1}, l_{1j_1}), (t_{2j_2}, l_{2j_2}), $\ldots$, (t_{sj_s}, l_{sj_s}), and

$G = T_1/t_{1j_1} + T_2/t_{2j_2} + \ldots + T_S/t_{Sj_S}$. This may happen for a finite number of values of parameter G; in this case, w and q_1, q_2, ..., q_s vary in finite ranges constrained by inequalities (6).

We are now ready to draw the MP curve. Apart from a finite number of values of parameter G (see Proposition 5(c)), w can assume only $m_1 + m_2 + \ldots + m_n = M$ values, to be precise the following values (see Propositions 1 and 2):

$$w = \frac{1}{l_{i1}} \quad i = 1, 2, \ldots, n$$

$$w = \frac{t_{ij} - t_{ij+1}}{l_{ij+1}t_{ij} - l_{ij}t_{ij+1}} \quad i = 1, 2, \ldots, n; \quad j = 1, 2, \ldots, m_i - 1$$

Let us call them $w_1, w_2, \ldots, w_M$, and let us number them in such a way that $w_1 \geq w_2 \geq \ldots \geq w_M$. The range in which labour may vary at each w_h, $\Delta L(w_h)$, is

$$\Delta L(w_h) = \begin{cases} \dfrac{l_{i1}T_i}{t_{i1}} & \text{if} \quad w_h = \dfrac{1}{l_{i1}} \\[3ex] \dfrac{l_{ij+1}T_i}{t_{ij+1}} - \dfrac{l_{ij}T_i}{t_{ij}} & \text{if} \quad w_h = \dfrac{t_{ij} - t_{ij+1}}{l_{ij+1}t_{ij} - l_{ij}t_{ij+1}} \end{cases}$$

from which we obtain:

$$L(w_h) = \sum_{k=1}^{h} \Delta L(w_k)$$

Thus, the MP curve is obtained by completing the step function

$$w = w(L) := w_h \text{ if } L(w_{h-1}) \leq L < L(w_h)$$

with vertical segments needed to have a continuous polygonal (obviously $L(w_0) = 0$). These vertical segments correspond to the cases in which the *post-factum* wage and the rates of rent vary in a range (see Proposition 5(c)). An example of the MP curve as a polygonal is drawn in Figure 1.2.

A complete analysis of a simple case in which both extensive and intensive rents are contemplated can be useful. Readers interested in simple cases in which only extensive rent or only intensive rent is analysed may consult Kurz and Salvadori (2015).

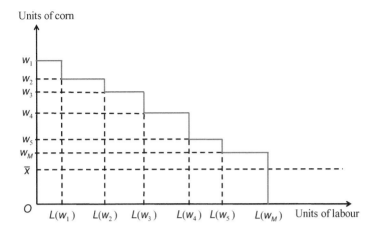

Figure 1.2 The *MP* curve as a polygonal.

Assume that there are two lands and three processes: (t_{11}, l_{11}), (t_{12}, l_{12}), (t_{21}, l_{21}) with $l_{11} < l_{21} < l_{12}$ (obviously $t_{12} > t_{11}$, otherwise process (t_{12}, l_{12}) would be dominated). Apart from a finite number of values of parameter G, w can assume only $m_1 + m_2 = 2 + 1 = 3 = M$ values, and to be precise the following values:

$$w_1 = \frac{1}{l_{11}}$$

$$w_2 = \frac{1}{l_{21}}$$

$$w_3 = \frac{t_{11} - t_{12}}{l_{12}t_{11} - l_{11}t_{12}}$$

The $\Delta L(w_h)$ are easily calculated:

$$\Delta L(w_1) = \frac{l_{11}T_1}{t_{11}}$$

$$\Delta L(w_2) = \frac{l_{21}T_2}{t_{21}}$$

$$\Delta L(w_3) = \frac{l_{12}T_1}{t_{12}} - \frac{l_{11}T_1}{t_{11}}$$

Hence if $0 < L < \Delta L(w_1)$, then $w = w_1$: any increment in production is obtained by increasing the cultivation of land 1; if $\Delta L(w_1) < L < \Delta L(w_1) + \Delta L(w_2)$, then $w = w_2$: any increment in production is obtained by increasing the cultivation of land 2; if $\Delta L(w_1) + \Delta L(w_2) < L < \Delta L(w_1) + \Delta L(w_2) + \Delta L(w_3)$, then $w = w_3$: any increment in production is obtained by decreasing the use of process (t_{11}, l_{11}) and increasing the use of process (t_{12}, l_{12}). If either $L = \Delta L(w_1)$, or $L = \Delta L(w_1) + \Delta L(w_2)$, or $L = \Delta L(w_1) + \Delta L(w_2) + \Delta L(w_3)$, w varies in ranges. To be more precise, w varies in range $w_2 \leq w \leq w_1$ if $L = \Delta L(w_1)$, in range $w_3 \leq w \leq w_2$ if $L = \Delta L(w_1) + \Delta L(w_2)$, and in range $w_3 \leq w \leq 0$ if $L = \Delta L(w_1) + \Delta L(w_2) + \Delta L(w_3)$.

Three remarks are appropriate. First, the *MP* curve is not a purely technological function: if two economies which share the same technology, that is the same processes, are endowed with different amounts of the various qualities of land, then they have different *MP* curves. Second, the *MP* curve is generally drawn as a concave function, but it does not need to be so. Third, with a finite number of processes, the *MP* curve must cut the horizontal axis unless there is a process producing corn without using land. With an infinite number of processes, the *MP* curve may approach the horizontal axis without cutting it. This happens, for instance, when there is an infinite sequence of processes, each of which uses a positive amount of land, but when the units of labour tend to infinity, the units of land (of some quality) tend to zero.

A further remark concerns the question of returns. Even if returns to scale are assumed to be constant from a technological point of view, the scarcity of land is reflected in returns that are *diminishing* (or *decreasing*). This means that there is no "law of diminishing returns" as a physical property, but[9]

diminishing returns must of necessity occur because it will be the producer himself who, for his own benefit, will arrange the doses of the factors and the methods of use in a descending order, going from the most favourable ones to the most ineffective, and he will start production with the best combinations, resorting little by little, as these are exhausted, to the worst ones.

(Sraffa, [1925, p. 288], 1998, p. 332)

It has become common to say that the lands are brought into cultivation following an order of fertility. And indeed such an order coincides with the sequence of inequalities (4). But this fact makes it crystal clear that what is called "fertility" in this context cannot be defined independently of technology and therefore is not just a physical property.[10]

1.3 On commodity inputs in the production of corn

In the previous two sections, I emphasized that capital consists only of wages advanced to workers at the beginning of the year and that there is no commodity input in corn production besides corn as a means of subsistence for workers. Why is this so? In this section, I will try to explain some difficulties connected with the presence of commodity inputs in the production of corn. For this purpose, I make use of a numerical example developed by Giuseppe Freni (1991; I benefited greatly from reading this paper).[11]

Let us assume an economy with only one quality of land that can be cultivated with three processes represented in Table 1.1. The available amount of land is 1. Inequalities analogous to inequalities (6) are as follows:

$$1 \le (1+r)\left(\frac{7}{10} + \frac{2}{5}\bar{x}\right) + \frac{1}{5}q$$

$$1 \le (1+r)\left(\frac{7}{24} + 2\bar{x}\right) + \frac{1}{2}q$$

$$1 \le (1+r)\left(\frac{21}{32} + \bar{x}\right) + \frac{1}{7}q$$

which may be written as (with symbols having obvious meanings)

Table 1.1 The input-output data of Freni's example

	Corn	Land	Labour		Corn
(1)	$\frac{7}{10}$	$\frac{1}{5}$	$\frac{2}{5}$	→	1
(2)	$\frac{7}{24}$	$\frac{1}{2}$	2	→	1
(3)	$\frac{21}{32}$	$\frac{1}{7}$	1	→	1

$$1 \leq (1+r)k_2 + \frac{1}{5}q$$

$$1 \leq (1+r)k_1 + \frac{1}{2}q$$

$$1 \leq (1+r)k_3 + \frac{1}{7}q$$

Obviously, k_1, k_2, and k_3 depend on $\bar{x}$. Let $\bar{x} = 1/6$, then $k_1 = 5/8$, $k_2 = 23/30$, and $k_3 = 79/96$. Then following the same procedure as in the previous section we get:

- if the existing amount of capital K is lower than $2k_1$, then only process (2) is operated, land is not fully cultivated, and $1 + r = 8/5$;
- if the existing amount of capital K exceeds $2k_1$ but is lower than $5k_2$, then processes (1) and (2) are operated together, land is fully cultivated and $1 + r = 36/31$;
- if the existing amount of capital K exceeds $5k_2$ but is lower than $7k_3$, then processes (1) and (3) are operated together, land is fully cultivated, and $1 + r = 192/185$.

Hence, a sort of *MP* curve may be built with capital, an amount of corn, measured along the horizontal axis and $(1 + r)$ on the vertical axis. Note that in this context $(1 + r)$ is not a pure number since it is actually multiplied by one unit of corn, and so it actually represents the marginal (gross) product of labour. Such a curve depends not only on technology and available land, like the *MP* curve of the previous section, but also on the real wage rate. However, the total product is still equal to the area below the "*MP* curve" and total rent is still equal to the area below the "*MP* curve" and above the horizontal straight line corresponding to the $(1 + r)$ of the last dose of capital employed. Yet "labour" and "capital" *are not proportional*, as in the previous two sections, and may even *move in opposite directions*. Indeed, if $2k_1 < K < 5k_2$, both the product and the capital increase if cultivation of land with process (2) is reduced and cultivation of land with process (1) is increased, keeping the total use of land constant, but process (1) uses much less labour (and much more corn as direct input) than process (2) and therefore the employment of labour is reduced. The diagram with $(1 + r)$ on the vertical axis and labour on the horizontal axis has the form depicted in Figure 1.3. This diagram does not allow one to ascertain total product, total rent, and total profit. Yet the fact that the relationship between labour and the rate of profits is not monotonic is significant.

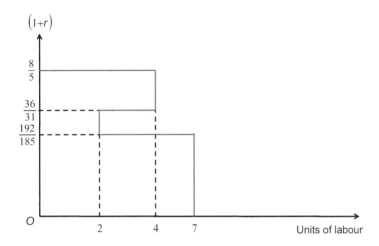

Figure 1.3 The curve relating labour to (1 + r).

The analysis developed in this section suggests that commodity inputs in the production of corn *can* be introduced into the picture, *provided they are proportional to labour*. Indeed if all processes have, instead of the form (1), the form

αl bushel of corn $\oplus$ t acres of land i $\oplus$ l hours of labour
$\rightarrow$ 1 bushel of corn

where α is *the same for all processes*, then there is an input of corn, but this input is proportional to the labour employed; a process can still be represented as (t_{ij}, l_{ij}); Section 1.2 can be confirmed in its integrity, but now w is not just the *post-factum wage*, but also includes commodity input and corresponding profit, that is $w = (1+r)(1+\alpha)\bar{x}$; all the results of Section 1.1 can be confirmed integrally, provided that what was there called wage bill is now called capital. In some sense, it is a question of taste: if readers consider the assumption that corn is produced without commodity inputs as less *ad hoc* than the assumption that corn is produced by commodity inputs that are strictly proportional to labour input, then the analysis developed in Sections 1.1 and 1.2 needs no change. On the contrary, if readers consider the assumption that corn is produced by commodity inputs that are strictly proportional to labour inputs as less *ad hoc* than the assumption that corn is produced without commodity inputs, then the analysis developed in Sections 1.1 and 1.2 can be modified as suggested here and the whole theory stays unchanged.

1.4 On the assumption of a given real wage rate[12]

To assume that the real wage rate is given and constant implies that the labour supply curve is horizontal and thus the demand for labour plays no role in wage determination. The latter can, of course, be justified only as a first step, a simplifying assumption. In fact, in some of his discussions with Malthus, Ricardo appears to have adopted this assumption precisely for the sake of convenience. It hardly needs to be stressed that to identify the Classical analysis of wage and population dynamics with the so-called "Iron Law of wages" is a travesty of the facts. Classical economists were aware that the relationship between economic growth, on the one hand, and wage and population dynamics, on the other, was far from linear. In their view, such a relationship actually differed both between different countries in a given historical period and between different historical periods of the same country, depending on a variety of cultural and institutional factors.

The Classical analysis of wage dynamics was open to historical, sociological, and institutional factors. Indeed in the Classical economists' concept of subsistence, wages did not mean just the consumption of the minimum amount of food and other basic commodities required by human physiology to keep workers and their families alive and in efficient working condition. Rather, subsistence wages included whatever commodity workers habitually consumed in a given country and at a given stage of economic development. Briefly stated, for Classical economists, habit was an attitude that had become a second nature (see Picchio, 1998; Stirati, 1998). One of the places where this 'open-ended' view of the natural rate of wages is very well expressed is in Torrens's *An Essay On the External Corn Trade* (1815). The relevant passage is worth quoting in full:

> The market price of labour is regulated by the proportion which, at any time, and any place, may exist between the demand and the supply; its natural price is governed by other laws, and consists, in such a quantity of the necessaries, and comforts of life, as, from the nature of the climate, and the habits of the country, are necessary to support the labourer, and to enable him to rear such a family as may preserve, in the market, an undiminished supply of labour. That the labourer must, usually, obtain for his work, a sufficient quantity of those things, which the climate

may render necessary to preserve himself, and such a family as may keep up the supply of labour to the demand, in healthful existence, is self-evident; and, *when we consider that things not originally necessary to healthful existence, often become so from use, and that men will be deterred from marriage, unless they have a prospect of rearing their families in the mode of living to which they have been accustomed, it is obvious, that the labourer must obtain, for his work, not only what the climate may render necessary, but what the habits of the country, operating as a second nature, may require.*

(Torrens, 1815, pp. 62–63, emphasis added)

Nevertheless, it must be stressed that even if higher rates of capital accumulation which presuppose higher rates of growth of the workforce require higher levels of the real wage rate, the basic logic of the argument illustrated in Section 1.1 by means of the assumption of a fixed real wage rate remains untouched: in normal conditions the pace at which capital accumulates regulates the pace at which labour grows.

Let us assume that higher growth rates of the labouring population require higher levels of the corn wage paid to workers. Higher wages give workers and their families access to more abundant and better nutrition and medical services. This reduces infant mortality and increases the average lifespan of workers. Let us assume that these facts may be represented by the function

$$\omega = h(g)$$

where $h(g)$ is the wage rate to be paid in order for the labouring population to grow at rate g, $h(g)$ is an increasing function, $h(0) = \bar{x}$, and $\bar{x}$ is the OW value seen in Figure 1.1. Let us further assume that the growth-profit mechanism is represented by function

$$g = \gamma(r),$$

where $\gamma(r)$ is an increasing function such that $\gamma(r_{\min}) = 0$. It is thus possible to determine a decreasing curve

$$\omega = \omega(L)$$

in Figure 1.1 that is above the horizontal straight line cutting the vertical axis at W in the segment OL_2 and is below it afterwards, where L_2 is such that

$$r_{\min} = \frac{MP(L_2) - \bar{x}}{\bar{x}}$$

Indeed from the equation

$$g = \gamma \left(\frac{MP(L) - h(g)}{h(g)} \right)$$

we obtain

$$MP(L) = h(g)\big(1 + \gamma^{-1}(g)\big),$$

where $\gamma^{-1}(g)$ is the inverse of function $\gamma(r)$. Note that the RHS is increasing in g, whereas the LHS is decreasing in L. Hence, the equation defines implicitly the decreasing function

$$g = g(L)$$

and

$$\omega = \omega(L) := h\big(g(L)\big)$$

is above the horizontal straight line cutting the vertical axis at W in the segment OL_2 and is below it afterwards. The resulting modifications to Figure 1.1 are here presented in Figure 1.4; they do not change the substance of the argument.

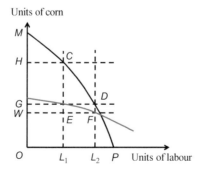

Figure 1.4 The MP curve and the ω curve (in red).

1.5 Endogenous growth[13]

A distinguishing feature of the model developed in Section 1.1 is the fact that the rate of capital accumulation is determined within the model. Growth of labour demand is one and the same thing as growth of the corn-capital advanced to workers, whereas growth of the labour supply is regulated by the pace at which capital accumulates, even if the 'Malthusian Law of Population' does not strictly hold. In other words, within Ricardo's theory of accumulation, labour is treated as a commodity that can be (re)produced. It differs from other produced commodities since it is not produced in a capitalistic way by a specific industry on a par with other industries, but is the result of the interplay between the fertility behaviour of the working population and historically given socio-economic conditions. Labour can thus set no limit on growth because it is 'generated' within the growth process. Only non-accumulable and non-producible factors of production may exert a limit to growth: as Ricardo made clear, these factors are natural resources in general and land in particular. In a nutshell, there is only endogenous growth in Ricardo. This growth is bound to lose momentum as the scarcity of natural factors of production makes itself felt in terms of extensive and intensive diminishing returns. (Technical change is of course envisaged to counteract these tendencies.)

For the sake of argument, let us try to imagine the Ricardian theory of growth without the problem of land. If there were no land and corn were produced by labour alone, then the MP curve of Section 1.1 would be constant whatever the amount of labour employed in corn production (see Figure 1.5).[14] Consequently, the growth rate would

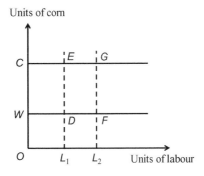

Figure 1.5 Corn produced by labour alone.

also be constant. The same idea can be found in Samuelson (1978, p. 1427f):

> If scarcity of land is ignored, the law of diminishing returns is negated and the [*MP*] becomes a horizontal line above the [*WF*]. This yields the perpetual exponential growth of Marx's *Tableau of Extended Reproduction*, with the growth arrows never shortening.

In Ricardo's words

> Profits do not necessarily fall with the increase of the quantity of capital because the demand for capital is infinite and is governed by the same law as population itself. They are both checked by the rise in the price of food, and the consequent increase in the price of labour. If there were no such rise, what could prevent population and capital from increasing without limit?
>
> (Ricardo, *Works*, VI, p. 301)

However, to assume that there is no land at all (and therefore there cannot be any landlords) is unduly restrictive. Consider instead an economy in which land does exist but is not an *indispensable* factor in corn production. This amounts to assuming that technology is such that processes are known in which corn is produced by labour alone without any land input.[15] The *MP* curve may be decreasing in a range, but it cannot be lower than the amount of corn needed to pay the *post-factum* wages of the workers employed in the cheapest process among those which produce corn without using land. The polygonal *MP* curve may be represented as in Figure 1.2, but the last segment is horizontal instead of vertical, and above the $\bar{x}$ horizontal line. In the case of continuous substitutability between labour and land, the *MP* curve may be continuously decreasing, but it is bounded from below. This case is illustrated in Figure 1.6, with the dashed line giving the lower boundary.

Finally, we may illustrate the case of increasing returns to labour. In order to be able to preserve the notion of a uniform rate of profits, it has to be assumed that the increasing returns are *external* to the firm and exclusively generated by the expansion of the market as a whole and the social division of labour, as Adam Smith had taught (*WN*, Chapters 1–3; see also Young, 1928; Kaldor, 1957). Ricardo was very conscious of this fact: "by a better division of labour... a million of men may produce double, or treble the amount... of 'necessaries, conveniences, and amusements,' in one state of society, that (sic) they

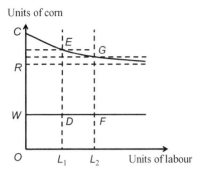

Figure 1.6 A backstop technology.

could produce in another" (*Works* I, p. 273). This may be modelled by assuming that there exist thresholds in the use of technology: some processes are available only if the labour employed is above a threshold. If there are many of these thresholds, the *actual MP* curve may be increasing, even if the calculation of total rent and total product requires a *fictitious MP* curve, namely an *MP* curve built on the assumption that the processes available after the threshold were available also before the threshold. Total product equals the area below the fictitious *MP* curve, and total rent equals the area below the fictitious *MP* curve and above the horizontal straight line cutting the fictitious (and the actual) *MP* curve at the unit of labour employed less productively. In the case of continuous substitutability between labour and land, we can define a *fictitious MP* curve as

$$MP = f(L, L^*),$$

where L represents the amount of labour employed, and the division of labour is artificially kept fixed at the level appropriate when the amount of labour employed is L^*. This function has all the formal properties of the *MP* curve used in Section 1.1. Yet the *actual MP* curve is

$$MP = f(L, L),$$

where $L^* = L$ and it may well be increasing (see Figure 1.7). Obviously, in the case of an increasing *actual MP* curve the stationary state is never obtained.

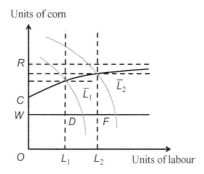

Figure 1.7 Increasing returns.

To conclude, it must be stressed that the patterns of endogenous growth studied in this section are essentially related to the fact that labour is envisaged as a commodity which is, so to speak, 'produced' by means of corn and nothing else. Accordingly, the real wage rate is considered "on the same footing as the fuel for the engines or the feed for the cattle".[16] The horizontal straight line cutting the vertical axis at W in Figure 1.1 can indeed be interpreted as the 'marginal cost function' related to the 'production' of labour. If the wage rate were to depend functionally on the amount of labour employed, then the marginal cost function would not be a horizontal straight line, but substantially the same argument would apply, as discussed in previous section. In a nutshell, the 'secret' of the endogeneity of growth in Ricardo consists in the assumption of a 'technology' producing labour.

1.6 A comparison with some models of the New Growth Theory

The mid-1980s, following the lead of Paul Romer and Robert Lucas, witnessed a formidable development of theoretical and empirical research into economic growth. This was also described as New Growth Theory (NGT) to indicate the claim to originality. The emphasis was on 'endogenous' mechanisms generating economic growth, that is, long-term growth determined 'within the model, rather than by some exogenously growing variables like unexplained technological progress' (Barro and Sala-i-Martin, 1995, p. 38). This is generally presented as the main theoretical difference between NGT and the 'old',

Solovian, growth theory, in which, as is well known, the economy's growth is related to two exogenously growing magnitudes, population and technical change.

In this section, an attempt will be made to relate some of the models of the NGT literature to the ideas that Ricardo developed about growth. It will indeed be argued that in a very precise sense the NGT can be said to involve a *return* to modes of thought and the method of analysis elaborated by classical authors. In terms of method, the NGT is a *long-period* theory, as the one advocated by Adam Smith and developed by David Ricardo. In terms of content, many of the models of the NGT dispense with the traditional neoclassical determination of the rate of profits in terms of the supply of and demand for capital. The following discussion attempts to clarify this fact.

Many models within NGT set aside all *non-accumulable* factors of production such as labour and land, and assume that all inputs in production are *accumulable*; that is, they are 'capital' of some kind. The simplest version of this class of models is the so-called '*AK* model', which assumes that there is a linear relationship between total output, *Y*, and a single factor capital, *K*, both consisting of the *same* commodity:

$$Y = AK,$$

where $1/A$ is the amount of that commodity required to produce one unit of itself. The rate of return on capital *r* is given by

$$r + \delta = \frac{Y}{K} = A,$$

where δ is the exogenously given rate of depreciation. The saving-investment mechanism jointly with the assumption of a constant rate of growth then determines a relationship between the growth rate, *g*, and the rate of profits, *r*.

Clearly, this model is akin to the model depicted here in Section 1.1 with a horizontal *MP* curve (see Figure 1.5). Note that the rate of profits is determined by technology alone and is totally independent of the interplay between demand and supply of capital. The model corresponds exactly to the argument developed in the previous section, i.e. the Ricardian theory of growth without the problem of land.

A slightly different path was followed by King and Rebelo (1990). Instead of one kind of 'capital', they assumed that there are two kinds, real capital, *K*, and human capital, *H*, both of which are accumulable. There are two lines of production: one for a physical good, used as a consumption good and as a real capital good, and the other for human capital. The production functions relative to the two lines of production are assumed to be homogeneous of degree one and strictly concave:

$$H = H\left(H_H, K_H\right) \tag{11.1}$$

$$K = K\left(H_K, K_K\right) \tag{11.2}$$

where H_H and K_H (H_K and K_K) are the human capital and the real capital used in the production of human (real) capital, respectively. Profit maximization implies that

$$\frac{\partial H}{\partial H_H} = r \tag{12.1}$$

$$\frac{\partial H}{\partial K_H} = \frac{r}{p} \tag{12.2}$$

$$\frac{\partial K}{\partial H_K} = rp \tag{12.3}$$

$$\frac{\partial K}{\partial K_K} = r \tag{12.4}$$

where r is the rate of profits and p is the price of human capital in terms of the commodity which is consumed or accumulated as physical capital (δ has been set equal to 0 in order to simplify the notation). Since functions (11) are homogeneous of degree one, their first derivatives are homogeneous of degree zero, and hence, the four equations (12) are enough to determine the four unknowns: r, p, H_H/K_H, H_K/K_K. The rate of profits is uniquely determined by the technology and profit maximization; the growth rate of the system is then endogenously determined by the saving-investment equation.

Comparing King and Rebelo (1990) with Ricardo's theory of accumulation as presented in this chapter, the following conclusion may be drawn: the role of *labour* in Ricardo is assumed by *human capital* in King and Rebelo (1990). Both factors of production are taken to be producible; with constant returns to scale, the rate of profits and, therefore, the rate of growth are determined and are constant over time. This is so because it is assumed that there is a 'tecnology' producing 'labour'. In order to make this fact palatable to a twentieth-century audience, the factor has been given a new name: human capital.

Two years prior to the publication of the paper by King and Rebelo (1990), Lucas (1988) had produced a paper, whose mechanism is very similar to that of King and Rebelo (1990), with the important difference that returns to scale are increasing because of the presence of an externality. Lucas (1988) assumed that the amount of labour, *N*, is either constant over time or is increasing at an exogenously given rate, but labour is just the support of human capital. Agents have a choice to make between two ways of spending their (non-leisure) time: to produce the physical good used as consumption or as physical capital or to accumulate human capital. The production function of the physical good is

$$Y = AK^\beta (uhN)^{1-\beta} h^{*\gamma}$$

and the 'production function' of human capital is

$$\dot{h} = \upsilon h(1-u)$$

where *K* is the physical capital, *u* is the proportion of time devoted to the production of the physical good, *h* is the existing amount of human capital, and h^* represents the externality: the single agent takes h^* as a parameter in his or her optimizing, but for society as a whole the accumulation of human capital increases output both directly and indirectly, that is, through the externality. It is immediately recognized that if there is no externality, that is if $\gamma = 0$, then Lucas' (1988) model is a variant of King and Rebelo's (1990) model. The externality adds a further source for endogenous growth. From a formal point of view, because of the externality, technology and profit maximization are not able to determine the rate of profits, but they are able to determine a relationship between the rate of profits and the rate of growth. Taking account of the saving-investment mechanism, which determines another relationship between the rate of profits and the rate of growth, these two variables are then determined simultaneously. Interestingly, increasing returns to scale are introduced in exactly the same way as in the previous section to justify an increasing *MP* curve (see Figure 1.7).

Other NGT models preserve the dualism between an accumulable and a non-accumulable input but restrict the impact of an accumulation of the former on its returns by modifying the production function. Jones and Manuelli (1990), for example, allow for both labour and capital, and even assume that technology is such that the marginal product of capital is a decreasing function of its stock, but it does not vanish as the amount of capital per worker tends to infinity. Jones and Manuelli assume that the per capita production function is

$$h(k) = f(k) + bk$$

where $f(k)$ is the conventional Solovian production function and b is a positive constant. As capital accumulates and the capital-labour ratio rises, the marginal product of capital falls, approaching asymptotically b, its lower boundary. This model is not much different from the model depicted here in Section 1.1 with an *MP* curve decreasing but bounded from below, like that of Figure 1.6 (of course we should also assume that $b > \bar{w} = OW$, otherwise the stationary state is obtained).

1.7 Concluding remarks

The main issue of this chapter is a very long-standing problem. Kaldor addressed it as early as 1955. What I have done here was first of all to provide some details and some assumptions that were not explicitly stated by Kaldor, but were needed to obtain his results. I also tried to connect the original presentation to other strands of literature and mainly to the so-called "new growth theory", that is, to the modern theory of endogenous growth. In so doing, I expanded the original model to take into account some special cases in which returns are not necessarily diminishing or even if they are, certain limits exist. With the exception of Section 1.2, these details are not exactly novelties and I have indicated how they are related to previous contributions.

1.A Mathematical appendix

The aim of this appendix is to prove four of the five propositions stated in Section 1.2 (indeed Proposition 3 does not require a proof). Before doing this I will prove that in general, given the processes $\left(t_{ij}, l_{ij}\right)$, $\left(t_{ij+u}, l_{ij+u}\right)$, $\left(t_{ij+v}, l_{ij+v}\right)$ with $0 < u < v$, process $\left(t_{ij+u}, l_{ij+u}\right)$ is not dominated if and only if

$$\left(l_{ij+u} - l_{ij}\right)t_{ij+v} + \left(l_{ij+v} - l_{ij+u}\right)t_{ij} > \left(l_{ij+v} - l_{ij}\right)t_{ij+u} \tag{A1}$$

As mentioned in Section 1.2, a process is dominated if it uses more inputs than a convex combination of other processes, i.e. process $\left(t_{ij+u}, l_{ij+u}\right)$ is not dominated if there is no $0 \leq \beta \leq 1$ such that

$$\beta t_{ij+v} + (1-\beta)t_{ij} \leq t_{ij+u} \quad \text{and} \quad \beta l_{ij+v} + (1-\beta)l_{ij} \leq l_{ij+u} \tag{A2}$$

This condition can be made more explicit in the following way. Because of inequalities (2) there is a single $0 < \lambda < 1$ such that

$$\lambda l_{ij+v} + (1 - \lambda) l_{ij} = l_{ij+u}$$

and therefore for $\beta \leq \lambda$ the second inequality (A2) is satisfied. Hence, both inequalities (A2) cannot be satisfied if and only if

$$\lambda t_{ij+v} + (1 - \lambda) t_{ij} > t_{ij+u}$$

that is

$$\frac{l_{ij+u} - l_{ij}}{l_{ij+v} - l_{ij}} t_{ij+v} + \frac{l_{ij+v} - l_{ij+u}}{l_{ij+v} - l_{ij}} t_{ij} > t_{ij+u}$$

Hence, process (t_{ij+u}, l_{ij+u}) is not dominated if and only if inequality (A1) holds.[17]

Proof of Proposition 1. Indeed $q_i = 0$ since land i is not fully cultivated (otherwise owners of uncultivated plots of land i would offer them at a lower rent); then equality (7) is a consequence of the fact that inequalities (6) must hold for every j and equality (5) must hold for some j since land i is cultivated; hence, process (t_{i1}, l_{i1}) and only process (t_{i1}, l_{i1}) is operated on land i; inequalities (8) are obvious since T_i / t_{i1} is the maximum amount of corn which can be produced on land i with process (t_{i1}, l_{i1}).

Proof of Proposition 2. Otherwise

$$w = \frac{t_{ij} - t_{ij+h}}{l_{ij+h} t_{ij} - l_{ij} t_{ij+h}}$$

$$q_i = \frac{l_{ij+h} - l_{ij}}{l_{ij+h} t_{ij} - l_{ij} t_{ij+h}}$$

because of equations (5) and process (t_{ij+1}, l_{ij+1}) cannot satisfy inequality (6):

$$q_i t_{ij+1} + w l_{ij+1} = \frac{l_{ij+h} - l_{ij}}{l_{ij+h} t_{ij} - l_{ij} t_{ij+h}} t_{ij+1} + \frac{t_{ij} - t_{ij+h}}{l_{ij+h} t_{ij} - l_{ij} t_{ij+h}} l_{ij+1}$$

$$= \frac{(l_{ij+h} - l_{ij}) t_{ij+1} + (t_{ij} - t_{ij+h}) l_{ij+1}}{l_{ij+h} t_{ij} - l_{ij} t_{ij+h}} < 1$$

The above inequality is a consequence of the fact that process $\left(t_{ij+1}, l_{ij+1}\right)$ is not dominated, and therefore inequality (A1) holds, and $0 < 1 < h$. Note that in this case equation (9) holds. Inequalities (10) are obvious since T_i/t_{ij} is the amount of corn which can be produced on land i when it is fully cultivated with process $\left(t_{ij}, l_{ij}\right)$.

Proof of Proposition 4. Otherwise there are lands h and k such that land $h > s$ is cultivated and land $k < s$ is not cultivated. As a consequence

$$w \le \frac{1}{l_{h1}}$$

$$q_k = 0$$

and process $\left(t_{k1}, l_{k1}\right)$ cannot satisfy inequality (6) because of inequalities (4).

Proof of Proposition 5. Indeed the unknowns to be determined are the s rents $q_1, q_2, \ldots, q_s$ and the *post-factum* wage rate w, since necessarily the other $n - s$ rents are nought. Moreover, at least one process for each land $1, 2, \ldots, s$ must be operated. This gives us s equations. The first $s-1$ lands are fully cultivated, otherwise cultivation of any plot of land s would contradict inequality (6) because of Proposition 1. If land s is not fully cultivated, then $q_s = 0$ and G may vary in a range: $G_{-s} \le G \le G_{-s} + T_s/t_{s1}$.[18] If land s is fully cultivated, then either two contiguous processes on any of the cultivated lands are operated and G may vary in a range ($G_{-i} + T_i/t_{ij} \le G \le G_{-i} + T_i/t_{ij+1}$) or only s processes are operated and $G = T_1/t_{1j1} + T_2/t_{2j2} + \ldots + T_s/t_{sjs}$.

Notes

1 On the debate concerning Ricardo and the 'corn model', see Ciccone and Trabucchi (2015).
2 This section owes much to a paper by Salvadori and Signorino (2017b).
3 An obvious implication of these assumptions (only one commodity exists and Say's Law holds) is that workers, landowners, and capitalists spend their entire income on corn. Kaldor, however, following the corn model interpretation, was less restrictive and mentioned that "To make the whole structure logically consistent it is necessary to suppose, not only that wages are fixed in terms of 'corn' but that they are entirely spent on 'corn' " (p. 86). On the other hand, Kaldor was less clear on landlords' and capitalists' consumption patterns: he assumed that the sum of rents and profits "is employed" outside the agricultural sector (*ibidem*). As we will see in the next chapter this vagueness cannot be maintained and Ricardo was aware of this fact.

4 What is meant by diminishing returns in agriculture will be clarified in Section 1.2.

5 Readers who have difficulty reading this section may benefit from first reading the paper by Kurz and Salvadori (2015), where extensive rent and intensive rent are dealt with separately and few remarks are devoted to the more general case in which both these forms of rent appear contextually.

6 For an attempt to analyze strategic behaviour on the part of the land owners, see Salvadori (2004).

7 In a comment sent to me, Giacomo Costa considers the distinction between the *post-factum* wage rate and the *ante factum* wage rate as crucial. He made a similar distinction in Costa (1985) in order to question "Kaldor-Pasinetti claim that in Ricardian theory distribution is logically prior to value, and that it is based on a 'surplus principle' which is foreign and alternative to the 'marginal principle' of neoclassical theory (see Kaldor, 1956, p. 84; Pasinetti, 1960, p. 81)." (Costa, 1985, p. 59, see also Morishima, 1989, p. 125). In the context of the present chapter the *post-factum* wage rate has the advantage to deal with the technology in a model with labour and land without material capital, without mentioning profit. On the other side, both Kaldor and Pasinetti use the 'marginal principle' to explain the income of landlords and the 'surplus principle' to explain the income of capitalists as a 'residuum'. Hence, Costa (1985) placed on this distinction a weight which, in my opinion, it cannot in fact support.

8 The proposition is stated and proved on the assumption that $l_{s-1,1} < l_{s,1}$. The case in which $l_{s-1,1} = l_{s,1}$ is left to the reader as an exercise.

9 The interested reader will greatly benefit from the reading of Sraffa (1925, 1998) on this issue.

10 Indeed if proper capital is introduced into the picture, the order in which lands are brought into cultivation generally depends also on distribution (see, for instance, Kurz and Salvadori, 1995, pp. 280–288, and the literature therein referred to).

11 The example is reproduced also in Kurz and Salvadori (1995, p. 313, Exercise 7.7). See also Freni (2018).

12 This section owes much to a paper by Kurz and Salvadori (2006). Some of the ideas contained in it can be found in Samuelson (1978, pp. 1426–1428). Let me give special thanks to Arrigo Opocher for this observation.

13 This section and the following one owe much to two papers by Kurz and Salvadori (1998b, 1999).

14 The theorist has no difficulty in making such an assumption, but the applied economist or the economic historian may consider that the land constraint is not binding (such as in North America in the early 1800s where there were large areas of land considered 'vacant and unappropriated').

15 The applied economist or the economic historian may consider that there are limited amounts of lands of high quality, but then there are large expanses of 'vacant and unappropriated' land. The historical example may still be North America in the early 1800s.

16 The reference is to Sraffa (1960, p. 9). In the first seven sections of his book Sraffa regarded wages as consisting in necessary subsistence only. In Section 8 he introduces the fact that wages may include a share of the surplus.

17 The same result is obtained by noting that for $\beta \geq \eta$ the second inequality (A2) is satisfied, where η is such that $\eta t_{ij+v} + (1-\eta)t_{ij} = t_{ij+u}$. As a consequence, both inequalities (A2) cannot be satisfied if and only if $\eta l_{ij+v} + (1-\eta)l_{ij} > l_{ij+u}$.

18 If $l_{s-1,1} = l_{s,1}$, these inequalities are mildly changed.

2 The two-sector model

Pasinetti (1960) rendered explicit the equations implicit in Kaldor's presentation of Ricardo's economics. The genesis of Pasinetti's paper is briefly recalled by Bellino (2015). Pasinetti drafted the paper in the academic year 1957–1958 while he was attending a series of seminars for graduate students at Harvard University. His main intellectual sources of inspiration were Kaldor's lectures at Cambridge in the previous academic year, Kaldor's (1955–1956) paper, and Sraffa's (1951) introduction to Ricardo's *Works*. In his original formulation, Pasinetti presented first the one-sector model, using equations instead of the diagram used by Kaldor, and then introduced another sector. However, Sraffa, to whom the paper was submitted for discussion, insisted on dropping the first part and starting directly with the two-sector model.

The simple fact that two commodities are taken into consideration introduces a number of questions that cannot be addressed in the one-commodity model. First of all the question of value: at what rate is one commodity exchanged with another? Second, the question of the distinction between agriculture and industry: are these two commodities both produced with land? Third, the distinction between necessaries and luxuries: are both commodities consumed by workers? And are both commodities consumed by landlords or by capitalists?

If only two commodities exist and we wish to have an agricultural commodity, an industrial commodity, a necessary good, and a luxury good, then there are only two alternatives: either the agricultural commodity is a necessary good and the industrial commodity is a luxury good or the agricultural commodity is a luxury good and the industrial commodity is a necessary good. As we will see, the assumption that the agriculture commodity is a necessary good whereas the industrial commodity is a luxury good is needed to obtain the Ricardian story of accumulation that converges to the stationary state. Consequently, this was the choice made by Pasinetti. It was an option that was close at hand, but it was also, in a sense, an obligatory choice. In this chapter, I will present the two-sector model of the Ricardian system. Hence, I assume that two commodities exist. I will refer to this model as the Pasinetti model. Let me emphasize that this chapter, as indeed is the case with the whole book, deals with what Ricardo called the "natural" course of the economy: technical change can counteract some of the tendencies discussed in this chapter. The model itself is presented in Section 2.1; Section 2.2 is devoted to analysis of the assumptions adopted in Section 2.1 concerning technology; Section 2.3 focuses on an analysis of the assumptions adopted in Section 2.1 concerning consumption; Section 2.4 compares the Pasinetti model with the Rebelo model, one of the contemporary endogenous growth models; Section 2.5 concludes the chapter.

2.1 The model[1]

Pasinetti analysed a closed economy in which there are two commodities, corn and gold, and three social classes, landlords, capitalists, and workers. Corn, the agricultural commodity, is produced by means of a diminishing returns technology that employs labour and land. Gold, the industrial commodity, is produced by means of a constant returns technology that employs only labour. Workers are assumed to spend the whole of their income (wages) only on corn, while landlords are assumed to spend the whole of their income (rents) only on gold. In order to simplify the presentation of the arguments, capitalists are assumed to spend the whole of their income (profits) on corn alone: capitalists buy corn both for capital accumulation and for personal consumption. Universal free competition and Say's Law of Markets obtain.

Calling the industrial commodity 'gold' is somewhat unfortunate, because it could give rise to associations that are potentially misleading. 'Gold' in Pasinetti (1960) is merely a name to indicate a manufactured product which, unlike the agricultural product 'corn', is not subject to diminishing returns and is a luxury good. But use of the word 'gold' for such a commodity has a problem: gold is generally associated with money, especially in Ricardo's writings. Thus, despite the fact that "A rose by any other name would smell as sweet", as William Shakespeare famously put it, and therefore the names of things do not affect what they really are, here I prefer to use the term 'silk cloth' or, more simply, 'cloth' instead of the word 'gold' used by Pasinetti. This will allow me to avoid any evocative element the reference to 'gold' may have. However, readers should be aware that much of the literature follows Pasinetti's nomenclature.

Pasinetti (1960) formalized technology in the two sectors by means of two simple production functions. As far as the agricultural sector is concerned, the physical quantity of corn produced, X_1, is a non-decreasing concave function of the number of workers employed in corn production, N_1:

$$X_1 = f(N_1), \tag{1.1}$$

$$f(0) \geq 0, \tag{1.2}$$

$$f'(0) > \bar{x}, \tag{1.3}$$

$$f''(N_1) < 0, \tag{1.4}$$

$$\lim_{N_1 \to \infty} f'(N_1) < \bar{x} \tag{1.5}$$

where $\bar{x}$ is the natural wage rate in terms of corn. Inequality (1.2) has an obvious meaning: even without using labour, land alone either produces a (small) amount of corn or produces nothing, but, taking inequality (1.3) into account, any (small) amount of labour is undoubtedly enough to produce some corn. Inequality (1.3) has a strong meaning: marginal productivity of labour is greater than the natural wage rate in terms of corn $\bar{x}$. This means that when a small amount of labour is employed in the production of corn, this labour is able to produce at least the amount of corn needed to pay labour at the wage rate $\bar{x}$ and, accordingly, the economy is viable. Without this assumption, the economy cannot reproduce itself, partly also because of inequality (1.4). The meaning of inequality (1.4) is clear: the marginal productivity of labour in agriculture is decreasing. If inequality (1.5) does not hold, the marginal productivity of labour is always higher than the real wage rate and therefore the stationary state does not exist. In effect, Pasinetti (1960, p. 87, eq. 20) introduced inequality (1.5) precisely in order to have the stationary state.

With regard to the industrial sector, Pasinetti (1960) assumed that the physical quantity of cloth produced, X_2, is proportional to the number of workers employed in cloth production, N_2:

$$X_2 = aN_2 \tag{2}$$

Hence, Pasinetti assumed that cloth is produced by labour alone. Thus, Pasinetti did not consider the existence of intermediate commodities or material capital. This is similar to what Kaldor did for the production of corn. However, whereas Kaldor's choice was obligatory, given the observations mentioned in Section 1.3, that of Pasinetti admits of another motivation. If both corn and cloth are produced without using material capital, then the labour theory of value holds and commodities are exchanged in proportion to their labour content. As Pasinetti (1960, p. 83, italics in the original) remarks "the value of the yearly product, *after deduction of rent*, is determined by the quantity of labour required to produce it". Hence, Pasinetti's contribution corresponds to the third stage described by Sraffa (1951), here mentioned in the introduction to Chapter 1, and clearly echoes it.

Obviously,

$$N = N_1 + N_2 \tag{3}$$

$$K = W = \bar{x}N, \tag{4}$$

where N is the total number of workers, W is the total wages bill, and K is the physical stock of 'capital' (both measured in terms of corn).

For each unit of labour employed, rent equals the difference between the product of that unit of labour and the product of the unit of labour employed less productively:

$$R = f\left(N_1\right) - N_1 f'\left(N_1\right) \tag{5}$$

where R is rents in terms of corn. Commodity prices are determined taking into account the fact that, under the usual assumption of free competition and absence of entry/exit barriers, the rate of profits, r, is uniform across sectors. In Ricardo's words,

> Whilst every man is free to employ his capital where he pleases, he will naturally seek for it that employment which is most advantageous; he will naturally be dissatisfied with a profit of 10 per cent., if by removing his capital he can obtain a profit of 15 per cent. This restless desire on the part of all the employers of stock, to quit a less profitable for a more advantageous business, has a strong tendency to equalize the rate of profits of all, or to fix them in such proportions, as may in the estimation of the parties, compensate for any advantage which one may have, or may appear to have over the other.
>
> (Ricardo, *Works*, I, pp. 88–89)

The implication is that

$$X_1 = R + (1+r)\bar{x}N_1 \tag{6.1}$$

$$X_2 p_2 = R + (1+r)\bar{x}N_2 \tag{6.2}$$

where corn is the numeraire, so that its price equals 1. Hence,

$$r = \frac{f'(N_1)}{\bar{x}} - 1$$

$$p_2 = \frac{f'(N_1)}{a} \tag{7}$$

The rate of profits r is determined by the conditions of corn production only, whereas the conditions of cloth production determine the price of cloth in terms of corn. After Sraffa (1960), we know that this is a consequence of the fact that corn, unlike cloth, is a basic commodity, needed directly or indirectly in the production of all commodities, whereas cloth is a non-basic.

At this stage, we can consider total labour employment N as an independent variable.[2] Accordingly, X_1 is determined by equation (1.1) once N_1 is determined. Similarly, X_2 is determined by equation (2) once N_2 is determined. In order to determine N_1 and N_2, we need to take into account that, given our assumptions on consumption patterns and Say's Law, the corn value of cloth produced equals rents:

$$aN_2 p_2 = f(N_1) - N_1 f'(N_1) \tag{8}$$

Hence,

$$N_2 = \frac{f(N_1) - N_1 f'(N_1)}{f'(N_1)}$$

and therefore,

$$N = N_1 + N_2 = \frac{f(N_1)}{f'(N_1)}.$$

Up to this point, we have closely followed the original algebraic formulation provided by Pasinetti. But the same results may be obtained graphically with a modified version of Kaldor's diagram. In Kaldor's original diagram, the unit of measure on the horizontal axis is labour and the unit of measure on the vertical axis is corn. We follow the same route, and therefore, the MP curve is immediately inserted into the diagram. The marginal product of labour in cloth production, measured in cloth, is a, but the same magnitude, measured in corn, is ap_2. Obviously, in equilibrium, the marginal product of labour in corn production must equal ap_2 — see equation (7) — and the rectangle with N_2 as width and ap_2 as height is exactly the amount of cloth produced measured in corn; consequently, it must equal the area under the MP curve and above the horizontal line ap_2 on the interval from zero to N_1 — see equation (8). This can easily be seen in Figure 2.1. We first insert N, $\bar{x}$, and the MP curve into the diagram. We then introduce the horizontal line ap_2 taking into account the fact that the intersection with the MP curve determines N_1 and $N_2 = N - N_1$, and therefore rent and the value in corn of the amount of cloth produced. Since these two magnitudes are the same, the horizontal line ap_2 must be drawn in such a manner as to ensure such equality.

In Figure 2.1, I have deliberately taken a value of N that could not be obtained if landlords were to spend their rents on corn as well as workers and capitalists. This means that landlords' consumption patterns play a significant role in determining the Ricardian stationary state.[3] Ricardo was acutely aware that capitalists' and landlords' consumption patterns had a significant impact on the workers' lot. In the famous Chapter XXXI, 'On Machinery', Ricardo wrote:

> the labouring class have no small interest in the manner in which
> the net income of the country is expended, although it should,

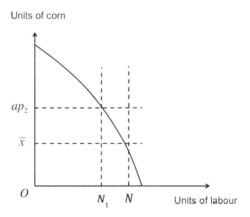

Figure 2.1 Kaldor's diagram for Pasinetti's Ricardian system.

in all cases, be expended for the gratification and enjoyments of those who are fairly entitled to it.

(Works I, p. 392)

Ricardo's claim will be further explored in Section 2.3.

All relations we found among variables are static in the sense that they do not refer to changes of variables over time. Pasinetti (1960, pp. 85–89) considered two dynamic processes: one concerning the wage rate (converging to the natural level) and the other concerning the rate of profits (converging to the minimum value accepted by the capitalists, that here equals zero). He assumed the former process to be faster than the latter. Such an assumption allowed him to analyse a model in which the former process has obtained its steady state, whereas the latter has not yet done so. Here we follow the same analytical procedure. Accordingly, we do not tackle the analytical difficulties inherent in treating the wage rate as an increasing function of the growth rate. This procedure is not very costly in terms of results (see Section 1.4). Pasinetti assumed that the derivative of capital with respect to time is a known increasing function of total profits. This relation can only be interpreted as a consequence of capitalists' preferences with regard to investment. Pasinetti does not attempt to specify this function. What he considered relevant was the fact that net investment is positive (and therefore the growth rate is positive) when profits are larger than a known threshold. In a

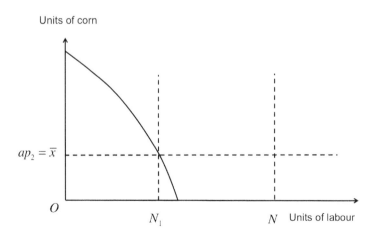

Figure 2.2 The stationary state in Kaldor's diagram for Pasinetti's Ricardian system.

footnote Pasinetti also refers to "a minimum rate of profit... necessary in order to induce capital accumulation" (p. 87f), but he never expresses this relationship in terms of rates instead of absolute values. Otherwise, he would have stated this relationship as

$$g = \gamma(r), \tag{9}$$

where $\gamma(r)$ is an increasing function such that $\gamma(r_{\min}) = 0$. This is the relationship we utilise in the following part of this book.

For the sake of simplicity let $r_{\min} = 0$. If $r > 0$, then g is positive, net investment is positive, capital is increasing over time as are the working population and number of workers employed in agriculture. Consequently, r and p_2 decline over time until $r = 0$, $ap_2 = \bar{x}$, and the growth rate is zero: the stationary state is obtained (see Figure 2.2).

2.2 On the production functions

Where does production function (equations 1.1–1.5) come from? The construction of this production function has been the subject of an exchange between Kurz and Salvadori (1992, 1998a) and Morishima (1996). Kurz and Salvadori (1992) constructed this function using linear programming in the footsteps of Freni (1991). The construction here proposed is, of course, equivalent to that proposed in 1992, but simpler since I use the analysis developed in Section 1.2.

From a mathematical point of view, the production function (1) is the integral of the *MP* curve, but actually we do not have to resort to integrals in order to build it. Suffice it to say that the height of the *MP* curve corresponds to the slope of the production function. More precisely, let us define

$$y_h = y_{h-1} + w_h \left[L(w_h) - L(w_{h-1}) \right]$$

with $y_0 = f(0)$, $L(w_0) = 0$, and let w_h and $L(w_h)$ be defined in Section 1.2. Then

$$f(N_1) := y_{h-1} + w_h \left[N_1 - L(w_{h-1}) \right] \text{if } L(w_{h-1}) \leq N_1 < L(w_h)$$

With respect to the production of cloth, there is no difficulty – such as that seen in Section 1.3 – in assuming that corn or even cloth itself is used in its production. However, calculations would be more cumbersome and the labour theory of value would no longer hold. Of course, the labour theory of value would not hold even if, following a suggestion at the end of Section 1.3, an input of corn proportional to the labour employed is introduced in the production of corn, unless an input of corn, in the same proportion to the labour employed, were to be introduced in the production of cloth as well.

An aspect that could be treated with respect to the technology for producing cloth concerns the question of returns in the production of industrial commodities. Echoing Adam Smith, Ricardo sometimes mentions the fact that returns could be increasing in the production of industrial commodities:

> The natural price of all commodities, excepting raw produce and labour, has a tendency to fall, in the progress of wealth and population; for though, on one hand, they are enhanced in real value, from the rise in the natural price of the raw material of which they are made, *this is more than counterbalanced* by the improvements in machinery, *by the better division and distribution of labour, and by the increasing skill*, both in science and art, *of the producers.*
>
> (*Works* I: 93–94, emphasis added)

Apart from the clear references to technical change, the reader cannot fail to recognize the reference to the division of labour and to learning by doing. A simple way to introduce increasing returns in the production of cloth could be to assume the existence of thresholds so that the product of cloth per unit of labour, a, is not constant as N_2 increases, but moves up as soon as a threshold is exceeded.

2.3 On workers' consumption

The fact that workers consume only corn implies that corn is the only basic commodity within Pasinetti's two-commodity model. The assumption concerning workers' consumption pattern is a crucial one in determining the Ricardian stationary state. Let us consider in this section a variant of the Pasinetti-Ricardo two-commodity model in which workers consume only cloth and landlords consume only corn. In this case, cloth becomes the only basic commodity of the model (while corn becomes non-basic) and, as a consequence, growth may not lose momentum. Within such a variant of the Ricardian two-commodity model, the rate of profits would be determined by the conditions of production of cloth only since equation (6.2) in this case reads:

$$ap_2 = (1+r)\bar{x}p_2 \qquad (10)$$

If also capitalists consume only cloth, then corn is not produced and, accordingly, no rent is to be paid to landlords. This ultra-modified Ricardian system (in which just one commodity, cloth, is produced and there are only two social classes, workers and capitalists) turns out to be a typical AK model, in the terminology used by modern endogenous growth theorists (see Section 1.6 and Figure 1.5). In order to preserve an economic role for landlords, we assume that capitalists consume corn so that corn is to be produced and rent is to be paid to landlords (thus, this modified model is still a two-commodity model).[4] However, this fact has no consequence for the rate of profits, which is determined uniquely by the conditions of production of cloth. Note that equation (7) still holds, since equation (6.1) is now written:

$$f(N_1) = f(N_1) - N_1 f(N_1) + (1+r)\overline{x}p_2 N_1,$$

The fact that capitalists consume corn but invest in cloth has two consequences. First, the relative size of the two sectors cannot be determined independently of the growth rate as in the previous section. Now we have

$$aN_2 = a(N - N_1) = (1+g)\overline{x}N \tag{11}$$

and therefore,

$$N_1 = \frac{a - (1+g)\overline{x}}{a} N \tag{12}$$

$$N_2 = \frac{(1+g)\overline{x}}{a} N$$

This is so since workers are paid at the beginning of the production period, whereas rents are paid at the end of the production period. In other words, wages are paid from capital, whereas rents are paid from revenue.

Second, the rate of return of an amount of capitalists' consumption good, ρ_C, is different from the rate of return on an amount of capital good, even if only the latter is what we call rate of profits, r. The rate of return on an amount of a commodity is calculated in this way. We start from such an amount and transform it in capital *at current prices.* Then the revenue of that capital is transformed again in the same commodity *at current prices.* Hence, the difference between the rate of profit and the rate of return on an amount of commodity is related to the change in prices. In the circumstances here analysed

$$(1+r)\left(1+\frac{\Delta p_2}{p_2}\right)=(1+\rho_C), \tag{13}$$

and since p_2 is not constant over time, because of the diminishing returns in agriculture, the two rates of returns are not equal. A problem that must be tackled is the following: is function (9) appropriate to attempt to capture capitalists' preferences with regard to investment? Or is a function like

$$g = \gamma(\rho_C), \tag{14}$$

where $\rho_C = r + (\Delta p_2 / p_2)(1+r) < r$ more appropriate? As we will see, both functions may have problems.

Let us first assume that equation (9) holds. Figure 2.3 allows us to make use of a diagrammatical exposition. We plot in the first quadrant the *MP* curve and *N*. Since the rate of profits is determined by equation (10) and the growth rate is determined by equation (9) and they are both constant over time, the green straight line in the fourth quadrant

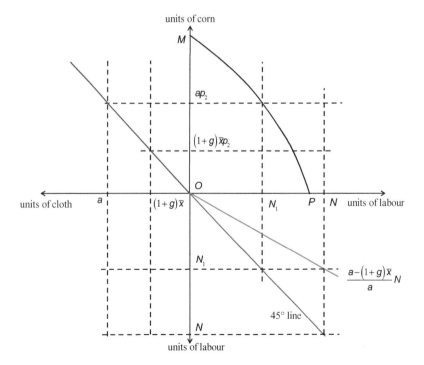

Figure 2.3 The Ricardian system in which workers consume cloth and the rate of growth is a function of *r*.

represents equation (12). Hence also N_1 (in the fourth quadrant) and ap_2 (in the first quadrant) are determined, also taking advantage of the 45° line in the fourth quadrant (the red straight line). By inserting a in the second quadrant, we get p_2 as the slope of the blue line in the second quadrant. By inserting $(1+g)\bar{x}$ into the third quadrant, we get the two equivalent rectangles $a(N - N_1)$ and $(1+g)\bar{x}N$.

Figure 2.3 may also be used to show what happens when N increases: N_1 increases and p_2 decreases. Since both r and g are constant, what happens when $N_1 = P$? The process must come to an end since N_1 cannot go beyond. As a consequence, either the MP curve never cuts the horizontal axis or the equation (9) cannot hold: it does not represent a reasonable behaviour of capitalists.

Let us assume now that equation (14) holds (and equation (9) does not). As a consequence, the growth rate may not be constant over time, despite the fact that the rate of profit is. Hence, it is convenient to expose the model in the form of difference equations. In particular, equations (7) and (10) still hold (but N_1 and p_2 are for N_{1t} and p_{2t}, respectively), whereas equations (9) and (11) need to be rewritten as

$$\frac{N_{t+1} - N_t}{N_t} = \gamma\left(r + \frac{p_{2t+1} - p_{2t}}{p_{2t}}(1+r)\right) \tag{15}$$

$$a(N_t - N_{1t}) = \bar{x}N_{t+1}, \tag{16}$$

respectively. Taking account of equations (7) and (10), equations (15) and (16) can be written as

$$\frac{N_{t+1} - N_t}{N_t} = \gamma\left(\frac{(1+r)f'(N_{1t+1}) - f'(N_{1t})}{f'(N_{1t})}\right) \tag{17}$$

$$N_{t+1} = (1+r)(N_t - N_{1t})$$

An explicit form of function $\gamma(\rho_C)$ could be

$$\gamma(\rho_C) = s(\rho_C - \rho_{C\min})$$

where s and $\rho_{C\min}$ are constants. In this case, equation (17) can be written as

$$\frac{N_{t+1}}{N_t} - (1 - s - s\rho_{C\min}) = s(1+r)\frac{f'(N_{1t+1})}{f'(N_{1t})}$$

I will not try to analyse this system.[5] Nevertheless, I will investigate the case in which the rate of return of an amount of capitalists' consumption good, ρ_C, is constant over time and therefore also the rate of growth of the price p_2, g_p, is constant over time as well as the growth rate of capital, g, and the proportion between N_1 and N_2. As a consequence,

$$p_{2t} = p_{20}\left(1 + g_p\right)^t$$

and therefore, because of equation (7),

$$f'\left(N_{10}(1 + g)^t\right) = ap_{20}\left(1 + g_p\right)^t$$

This may hold if and only if function (1.1) is a Cobb-Douglas, that is if and only if function (1.1) has the format

$$X_1 = BN_1^\alpha$$

where $B > 0$ and $0 < \alpha < 1$ are constants. Note that α relates g and g_p:

$$\left(1 + g\right)^{\alpha - 1} = 1 + g_p$$

An undesirable property is that land is of a single quality and only intensive rent exists. Moreover, we would observe the euthanasia of the capitalists since their consumption would go to zero: the whole production of corn would tend to be consumed by the landlords when N_1 tends to infinity. The same thing happens also when equation (9) holds (and equation (14) does not). Indeed when $N_1 = P$, capitalists' consumption is zero. In both cases, this is a consequence of the fact that the price of cloth is (or tends to) zero.

2.4 Comparison with an NGT model

Rebelo (1991) introduced a New Growth Theory (NGT) model in order to show that increasing returns are not necessary to obtain endogenous growth and that it is enough to assume that the capital goods which are indispensable in production can themselves be produced without the direct or indirect contribution of factors that cannot be accumulated, such as land (an argument which may seem obvious to scholars who know the difference between basic and non-basic commodities introduced by Sraffa 1960). In the Rebelo model, there are two types of factors of production: reproducible, which can be accumulated over time (e.g., physical and human capital), and non-reproducible, which are available in the same quantity in every period (e.g., land). The economy has two sectors of production: a consumption sector and a capital sector. The capital sector uses the fraction $(1-\phi_t)$ of the available capital stock Z_t to produce investment goods with a technology that is linear in the capital stock:

$$I_t = A(1-\phi_t)Z_t$$

The consumption sector combines the remaining capital stock with non-reproducible factors T to produce consumption goods. The production function of the consumption industry is assumed to be Cobb-Douglas:

$$C_t = B(\phi_t Z_t)^\alpha T^{1-\alpha}$$

Are these production functions equivalent to those used in previous section? Certainly they are. First of all T is constant and $T^{1-\alpha}$ can be incorporated into parameter B, so that the production function incorporates, as we saw in Section 1.2, not only purely technical elements, but also availability of land. Note, however, that land is of a single quality so that only intensive rent can be contemplated and extensive rent cannot. Second, we define $\bar{x}N = Z_t$, $N_1 = \phi_t N$, and $N_2 = (1-\phi_t)N$. Therefore,

$$A(1-\phi_t)Z_t = \frac{a}{\bar{x}}(1-\phi_t)Z_t = aN_2$$

$$B(\phi_t Z_t)^\alpha = F(\phi_t Z_t) = f\left(\phi_t \frac{Z_t}{\bar{x}}\right) = f(N_1)$$

Hence with respect to technology, the only difference is that Rebelo assumes a specific production function for the consumption good and Pasinetti does not. The other difference is that the consumption good of Rebelo is the commodity consumed by landlords and capitalists in the model of the previous section; consumption of workers does not appear as such: it is capital.

In the Rebelo model, the economy has a constant population composed of a large number of identical agents who seek to maximize utility, defined as

$$U = \int_0^\infty e^{-\rho i} \frac{C_t^{1-\sigma}-1}{1-\sigma}$$

but this is used just to determine the relationship

$$g_{ct} = \frac{r_{ct} - \rho}{\sigma},$$

where g_{ct} is the growth rate of consumption and r_{ct} is the rate of interest for loans denominated in the consumption good. This is an important difference in terms of analytical tools since we may be sure that Pasinetti never thought to describe the saving-investment mechanism by means of an everlasting representative agent. Pasinetti only assumed that the saving-investment mechanism determines an increasing function between the rate of profits and the growth rate. But at the end of the story Rebelo finds a very specific relationship of this type. So we can just assume this relationship and dispense with any reference to its microfoundation.

The two stories then follow in a very similar way since, in order to maximize profits, firms have to be indifferent about employing their marginal unit of capital to produce either consumption goods (corn) or capital goods (cloth), that is equation (8) or the equivalent we can write with Rebelo's formalism. There is only some particular attention by Rebelo to connect the rate of interest for loans denominated in the consumption good (corn) to the rate of interest for loans denominated in the capital good (cloth). The standard arbitrage argument applies[6]:

$$r_c = r_z + g_p,$$

where g_p is the growth rate of the price of cloth (the capital good). For Pasinetti, and for the model of the previous section, what is called growth rate is termed g_z by Rebelo and is the growth rate of capital, which is also the growth rate of labour; similarly what is called rate of profits by Pasinetti is the rate of interest for loans denominated in the capital good for Rebelo. Hence, the attention by Rebelo we have noticed is related to the particular saving-investment mechanism that he uses, based on the everlasting representative agent. This is equivalent to assuming equation (14) (and not equation (9)).

The comparison between Pasinetti's (1960) model, formalizing Ricardian growth theory, and Rebelo's (1991) model, which is one of the simplest models developed within the 'new' growth theory, was provided by D'Alessandro and Salvadori (2008). They show that both models share the same structure in the sense that they consist of the same set of equations, even if the interpretation given to these equations and to the symbols involved may be different. This result enforces the thesis according to which many endogenous growth models have an undeniable 'Classical' flavour. Indeed, the small changes concerning the assumed pattern of consumption of the three social classes in the Pasinetti model are sufficient to obtain the model developed by Rebelo (1991) within the NGT literature. Since the Classical derivation of the model investigated by Pasinetti (1960) is undisputed, the analysis presented by D'Alessandro and Salvadori confirms the claim made in a number of papers by Kurz and Salvadori (1998b, 1999, 2003) that the logical structure of some of the models developed within the NGT literature is substantially 'Classical'. As clarified in Section 1.6, these models do not determine the rate of profits in terms of the demand and supply of something called 'capital', but in terms of a 'technology' producing 'human capital' or 'knowledge', a procedure which is analytically equivalent to the assumption of a given real wage rate adopted by the Classical economists. What D'Alessandro and Salvadori (2008) did not recognize was the important role that the choice of a production function of Cobb-Douglas type played in the story: without that assumption the growth rates would not have been constant over time.

2.5 Concluding remarks

The main issue of this chapter, formulated by Pasinetti as early as 1960, has thus been known for quite some time. What I have done here was to provide some details and clarify the role of some assumptions: although they are explicitly invoked by Pasinetti, their role was not always crystal clear. Analysis of the assumptions concerning the technology involved in producing corn was central in a debate during the 1990s (see Kurz and Salvadori 1992 and 1998a, Morishima 1996). The analysis of assumptions concerning consumption is more recent and is presented here for the first time, though many relevant aspects – but not all – have already been clear for a decade or so (see D'Alessando and Salvadori, 2008). I was also keen to elaborate a graphical representation in the footsteps of Kaldor (see Salvadori and Signorino, 2017b). In addition, I tried to connect the Pasinetti model to another strand of the literature, namely that of the models developed within the modern theory of endogenous growth (see D'Alessando and Salvadori, 2008).

Notes

1 This section is indebted to a paper by Salvadori and Signorino (2017b).
2 Here we follow a different route from that adopted by Pasinetti, who took K as given: see eq. 16 of Pasinetti (1960, p. 84).
3 Bellino and Nerozzi (2017) analyse the interesting case in which landlords spend only a fraction $(1 - \beta)$ of their rents on cloth (actually gold) and the

remaining fraction β on corn. They show that "the fundamental variables of the system, that is, rents, profits, the rate of profits and the price of corn, will change with β, that is, with changes of final demand" (p. 12).

4 An alternative route is followed by Fiaschi and Signorino (2003) who analyse the relationship between income distribution and consumption patterns in a Classical growth model and show that both the take-off of an agricultural economy and the long-run growth of an industrialized economy depend on the expenditure patterns of the various social classes (see also Fiaschi and Signorino, 2006).

5 It can be shown, however, that it generates chaotic movements when the MP curve cuts the horizontal axis, but this is no surprise (see Bhaduri, A. and Harris, D., 1987). Indeed, if

$$\lim_{t \to \infty} \frac{f'(N_{1t+1})}{f'(N_{1t})} = 1$$

then

$$\lim_{t \to \infty} \frac{N_{t+1}}{N_t} - 1 = s(r - \rho_{C\min})$$

and therefore N_t approximates the function

$$N_t = A\left[1 + s(r - \rho_{C\min})\right]^t$$

where A is a constant of integration. As a consequence, we obtain by equation (17) that N_{1t} approximates the function

$$N_{1t} = N_t - \frac{1}{1+r} N_{t+1} = \frac{r - s(r - \rho_{C\min})}{1+r} N_t$$

6 The difference with regard to equation (13) is related to the fact that in Rebelo the time is continuous whereas in the previous section it is discrete.

3   The small open economy

The economies we have studied in the previous two chapters are closed. A *closed* economy is an economy that has no trade or financial relationships with other economies. At first sight, it may appear quite odd to assume the existence of a closed economy in an interdependent world such as that in which Ricardo lived and, even more so, the globalized world in which we live. A more in-depth reflection suggests that the assumption is less bizarre than it may appear at first sight. For instance, planet Earth is a closed economy. Moreover, by political decision, a given country at a given time may decide to sever all of its trade and financial interconnections with other countries and adopt a strict autarkic policy or may be forced into an autarkic policy by an embargo or a blockade imposed by other countries. However, many interesting economic problems cannot be analysed within the framework of a closed economy. Accordingly, in this chapter we engage in the analysis of an *open* economy, namely, an economy trading with other economies.

The introduction of international trade entails a number of analytical difficulties. Attempts have therefore been made to avoid such complications. The most obvious attempt consists in obtaining policy insights from the analysis of a closed economy. Ricardo himself was not totally averse to this attitude. Another attempt consists in analysing an open economy without considering the mutual relationships among trading economies. This is the 'small open economy' assumption, an assumption that is obviously partially misleading, but has a clear analytical advantage: it simplifies the analysis of a number of properties characterizing an open economy. It goes without saying that the 'small open economy' assumption is merely a useful simplifying hypothesis to be subsequently removed in order to study the analytical properties of a 'world economy', an economy in which several open countries freely trade among themselves. This is the route that we follow in this chapter, devoted to the analysis of a small open economy.

The term 'small' does not refer to the genuine size of the economy, measured on the basis of its population or national income. A *small open economy* is an economy whose inhabitants (including the government and any decision-maker) have no effect on the relative prices at which commodities are exchanged in the world market. Hence, a small open economy is an economy whose inhabitants face *given* international prices. As we will see, some misleading results may be obtained because of the assumption of given and constant international prices. To overcome such potentially misleading results, we need an analysis of the world economy in which international prices are determined by trade relationships among the existing open economies. This is what will be done in the next two chapters.

This chapter may also be useful to complete the characterization of David Ricardo as an endogenous growth theorist. Ricardo considered the opening of England to the international corn market as a way to introduce an indefinite period of capital accumulation and population growth. In support of his approach, he used arguments that are in many respects very similar to those of modern theorists of endogenous growth. Section 3.1 of this chapter is devoted to a brief anthology concerning 'Ricardo on international trade and long-run growth'. The model is then presented in Section 3.2; Sections 3.3 and 3.4 are devoted to an analysis of gains from trade; Section 3.5 is devoted to signalling the misleading results mentioned above; Section 3.6 concludes the chapter.

3.1 Ricardo on international trade and long-run growth[1]

In a letter dated 18 December 1814, Ricardo wrote to Malthus:

> Accumulation of capital has a tendency to lower profits. Why? because every accumulation is attended with increased difficulty in obtaining food, unless it is accompanied with improvements in agriculture; in which case it has no tendency to diminish profits. If there were no increased difficulty, profits would never fall, because there are no other limits to the profitable production of manufactures but the rise of wages. *If with every accumulation of capital we could tack a piece of fresh fertile land to our Island, profits would never fall.* I admit at the same time that commerce, or machinery, may produce an abundance and cheapness of commodities, and if they affect the prices of those commodities on which the wages of labour are expended they will so far raise profits.
>
> (*Works* VI, p. 162, emphasis added)

The first part of the quotation is a clear summary of the results of the previous two chapters, concerning a closed economy. The counterfactual of new fertile land introduces the fact that 'commerce, or machinery' may change the direction of profit movements. But this change is introduced with a metaphor and not yet with a proper analysis. The assimilation of commerce and machinery, of international trade and technical change, is remarkable. Modern endogenous growth theorists stress the role of technical change, whereas Ricardo assigns greater emphasis to international trade.

The counterfactual of new fertile land added to the British Isles in the process of capital accumulation was a recurring theme in the Malthus-Ricardo correspondence of late 1814–mid-1815 (see, for instance, *Works* VI: 168–169, 217–218 and 220). The same counterfactual was used by Ricardo in *An Essay on Profits* (1815; *Works* IV: 1–41), the first systematic work in which Ricardo publicly presented his theory of profits:

> Profits of stock fall only, because land equally well adapted to produce food cannot be procured; and the degree of the fall of profits, and the rise of rents, depends wholly on the increased expense of production: *If, therefore, in the progress of countries in wealth and population, new portions of fertile land could be added to such countries, with every increase of capital, profits would never fall, nor rents rise.*
>
> (*Works* IV, p. 18, emphasis added)

In Ricardo's view, British growth prospects in the aftermath of the Napoleonic Wars crucially depended on an economic policy variable, the foreign corn trade legislation to be enacted by the British Parliament. *Contra* Malthus who endorsed a protectionist food policy in *The Grounds of an Opinion on the Policy of Restricting the Importation of Foreign Corn* (1815), Ricardo in *An Essay on Profits* argued that free-trade equilibrium is characterized by a more efficient allocation of overall British capital between the two productive sectors of the British economy (agriculture and manufactures) and by a higher rate of growth than autarky equilibrium (see Salvadori and Signorino, 2015):

> we may contemplate an increase of prosperity and wealth, far exceeding that of any country which has preceded us. This may take place under either system, that of importation or restriction, though not with an equally accelerated pace, and is no argument why we should not, at every period of our improvement, avail ourselves of the full extent of the advantages offered to our acceptance – it is

no reason why we should not make the very best disposition of our capital, so as to ensure the most abundant return.

(*Works* IV, p. 34)

As is well known, the close relationship between free international corn trade and the domestic rate of profits was later emphasized by Ricardo in Chapter VII, 'On Foreign Trade', of his *Principles*:

> It has been my endeavour to shew throughout this work, that the rate of profits can never be increased but by a fall in wages, and that there can be no permanent fall of wages but in consequence of a fall of the necessaries on which wages are expended. If, therefore, by the extension of foreign trade, or by improvements in machinery, the food and necessaries of the labourer can be brought to market at a reduced price, profits will rise. *If, instead of growing our own corn, or manufacturing the clothing and other necessaries of the labourer, we discover a new market from which we can supply ourselves with these commodities at a cheaper price, wages will fall and profits rise*; but if the commodities obtained at a cheaper rate, by the extension of foreign commerce, or by the improvement of machinery, be exclusively the commodities consumed by the rich, no alteration will take place in the rate of profits.
>
> (*Works* I, p. 132, emphasis added)

Here Ricardo abandons the metaphor for a theory. The analysis of the small open economy is introduced to show that at the *current* international prices, it pays England to import cheap foreign corn in order to reduce its domestic labour cost and increase its domestic rate of profits. Nevertheless, the analysis is very England-centric, so to speak. Ricardo does not seem to be interested in providing a fully developed analysis of the consequences that international trade entails and explicitly puts aside the consequences that international trade implies for the profit rate of corn-exporting countries. Even the last sentence in the above quotation concerns the fact that the importing of 'commodities consumed by the rich' does not have the same beneficial effect on the *British* rate of profit. Once again, the equivalence between 'the extension of foreign commerce' and 'the improvement of machinery' is remarkable.[2]

Ricardo, in *The Funding System* (1820), explicitly considered international trade as a way out of the gloomy destiny of the stationary state:

> When the land of a country is brought to the highest state of cultivation, when more labour employed upon it will not yield in return

more food than what is necessary to support the labourer so employed, that country is come to the limit of its increase both of capital and population. *The richest country in Europe is yet far distant from that degree of improvement, but if any had arrived at it, by the aid of foreign commerce, even such a country could go on for an indefinite time increasing in wealth and population, for the only obstacle to this increase would be the scarcity, and consequent high value, of food and other raw produce.* Let these be supplied from abroad in exchange for manufactured goods, and it is difficult to say where the limit is at which you would cease to accumulate wealth and to derive profit from its employment.

(*Works* IV, p. 179, emphasis added)

The modern reader may appreciate the reference to 'an *indefinite* time increasing in wealth and population', akin to the perpetual growth mentioned by the modern endogenous growth theorists. Ricardo is in a sense more realistic than contemporary theorists since he refers to an *indefinite* period of time. But this is comprehensible: Ricardo knows, of course, that his analysis is related to the *given* international prices, and such prices cannot be constant forever.

In the course of a session of Parliament devoted to 'Agricultural Distress' (May 30, 1820), Ricardo is reported to have claimed that "This would be the happiest country in the world, and *its progress in prosperity would be beyond the power of imagination to conceive*, if we got rid of two great evils – the national debt and the corn laws" (*Works* V: 55, emphasis added). Finally, in his 1822 pamphlet, *On Protection to Agriculture*, Ricardo warned his readers that a protectionist food policy would artificially raise the domestic price of corn and the rate of wages, thus depressing the domestic rate of profits and capital accumulation (*Works* IV: 235–241; see also Maneschi, 2015).

This leaves us in no doubt: Ricardo was a deep-rooted endogenous growth theorist!

3.2 The model[3]

Given the significance of international trade within Ricardo's economics, Salvadori and Signorino (2016) proposed an open economy variant of Pasinetti's 1960 model in which the economy under scrutiny was a small open one. In that paper, besides a rational reconstruction and assessment of the relevant part of Ricardo's views on international corn trade and his debate with Malthus, Salvadori and Signorino showed that a small open economy may grow forever. The assumption of a small open economy does not correspond to the Great Britain that Ricardo had in mind when he wrote his *An Essay on Profits*.[4] However, such an assumption is the simplest one to make in order to clarify that international trade may be considered a mechanism capable of performing the task set out by Ricardo. The argument was not totally new. In particular, Findlay (1974), commenting on Pasinetti's (1960) paper, remarked that (see also Maneschi, 1983, 1992; Burgstaller 1986):

> The analysis of the effects of international trade can also be carried out on the basis of the "small country" assumption that the world terms of trade are exogenously determined. In this connection, it is interesting to note that an increase of productivity in [cloth]... would... lead to a diversion of labour from corn to [cloth] for export, relative product prices being determined by the world market, and hence to a rise in the rate of profits and a decline in rent.
>
> (Findlay, 1974, p. 13)

These observations notwithstanding, a Ricardian model *à la* Pasinetti with international trade was proposed for the first time by Salvadori and Signorino (2016) and, although the intuition has long been around, it had never been formally shown that such a model may generate endogenous growth.

The obvious difference between a closed and an open economy is that, in the former, corn and cloth can only be produced domestically, while in the latter it is also possible to import corn or cloth from abroad. In short, international trade is a kind of 'technology' to obtain commodities by means of exchange instead of domestic production.[5] Formally, while in Pasinetti's closed economy there are only two commodities and two technological processes, in a small open economy we have two commodities and four processes:

i   domestic production of corn devoted to the domestic consumption of corn
ii domestic production of corn devoted to export in order to import foreign cloth
iii domestic production of cloth devoted to the domestic consumption of cloth
iv domestic production of cloth devoted to export in order to import foreign corn

Since in the study of a small open economy international prices are considered as given, besides the production functions,

$$X_1 = f(N_1), \tag{1.1}$$

$$f(0) \geq 0, \tag{1.2}$$

$$f'(0) > \bar{x}, \tag{1.3}$$

$$f''(N_1) < 0, \tag{1.4}$$

$$\lim_{N_1 \to \infty} f'(N_1) < \bar{x}, \tag{1.5}$$

$$X_2 = aN_2, \tag{2}$$

which are the functions (1) and (2) discussed in Chapter 2, we also have the following 'production functions'

$$I_1 = \bar{p}_2 a N_{I1}, \tag{3.1}$$

$$\bar{p}_2 a > \bar{x}, \tag{3.2}$$

$$I_2 = \frac{f(N_{I2} + N_1) - f(N_1)}{\bar{p}_2}, \tag{4}$$

where I_1 is the quantity of corn imported; N_{I1} is the quantity of labour employed in the production of cloth that is exported to import foreign corn; $\bar{p}_2$ represents the terms of trade between cloth and corn, namely the ratio of the international price of cloth to the international price of corn; I_2 is the quantity of cloth imported; and N_{I2} is the quantity of labour employed in the production of corn that is exported in order to import foreign cloth. Equations (3.1) and (4) imply that the import-export activity does not require time and there are no transportation costs: the cloth produced for exportation, aN_{I1}, is immediately transformed into imported corn, I_1, and the corn produced in order to be exported, $f(N_{I2} + N_1) - f(N_1)$, is immediately transformed into imported cloth, I_2. Inequality (3.2) has the same role as the analogous inequality (1.3): any economy in which corn is imported would not otherwise be viable, i.e. it would not be able to reproduce itself. More precisely, in the stationary state in which $\bar{p}_2 a \leq \bar{x}$, corn could not be imported either because its international price would be too high, in comparison to the price of cloth, or because labour productivity in cloth production would be too low. Obviously

$$N = N_1 + N_2 + N_{I1} + N_{I2} \tag{5}$$

Additional assumptions on technology are required in order to ensure that the model is of interest in this context. If $a\bar{p}_2 \geq f'(0)$, it will always be preferable to import foreign corn rather than produce it domestically, since the labour cost of the cloth needed to import it would always be lower than the cost of producing it domestically. As a consequence, corn is never produced domestically and the economy is actually a single commodity economy, with no rent and no landlords. On the other hand, if

$$\lim\nolimits_{N_1 \to \infty} f'(N_1) \geq a\bar{p}_2, \tag{6}$$

it will always be preferable to produce corn domestically rather than to import it, since the labour cost of the cloth needed to import it would be higher than the cost of producing it domestically. As a consequence, cloth is never produced domestically and the economy is actually a single commodity economy as in the case analysed by Kaldor (see Chapter I). The only difference would be that in Kaldor's model landlords consumed corn, whereas in this model exactly the same amount of corn is exported in order to import the foreign cloth consumed by landlords. In order to avoid the simple case in which only cloth is produced domestically at any time, the assumption of inequality (1.3) is substituted by the assumption of inequality

$$f'(0) > \bar{p}_2 a, \tag{1.6}$$

which implies inequality (1.3) because of inequality (3.2). No other change is needed to avoid the simple case in which only corn is produced domestically at any time, i.e. that inequality (6) holds, since inequalities (1.5) and (3.2) prevent inequality (6) from holding.

Let us summarize in Table 3.1 the input-output conditions of the four processes involved in a small open economy.

Processes (1) and (2) produce corn, and processes (3) and (4) produce cloth. Processes (1) and (3) are domestic, and processes (2) and (4) operate through trade. Processes (1) and (4) use land, and processes (2) and (3) do not. It is readily recognized that corn is the only basic commodity since no cloth is used in the production of corn, whereas corn is used in the production of cloth, inasmuch as it is the wage-good consumed by workers employed in the cloth sector.[6] As a consequence, the rate of profits r is determined only by the conditions of corn production which, in turn, depend on the conditions of cloth production:

$$r = \max\left\{\frac{f'(N_{I2} + N_1)}{\bar{x}}, \frac{a\bar{p}_2}{\bar{x}}\right\} - 1 \tag{7}$$

Table 3.1 Input-output conditions

Processes	Corn		Corn	Cloth
(1)	$\dfrac{\overline{x}}{f'\left(N_{I2}+N_1\right)}$	$\rightarrow$	1	–
(2)	$\dfrac{\overline{x}}{a\overline{p}_2}$	$\rightarrow$	1	–
(3)	$\dfrac{\overline{x}}{a}$	$\rightarrow$	–	1
(4)	$\dfrac{\overline{x}p_2}{f'\left(N_{I2}+N_1\right)}$	$\rightarrow$	–	1

On the contrary, the conditions of cloth production determine only the price of cloth:

$$p_2 = \min\left\{\frac{\overline{x}}{a}(1+r), \frac{\overline{x}p_2}{f'\left(N_{I2}+N_1\right)}(1+r)\right\} \tag{8}$$

Hence if $a\overline{p}_2 \leq f'\left(N_{I2}+N_1\right)$, then

$$r = \frac{f'\left(N_{I2}+N_1\right)}{\overline{x}} - 1 \tag{9.1}$$

$$p_2 = \frac{\overline{x}p_2}{f'\left(N_{I2}+N_1\right)}(1+r) = \overline{p}_2, \tag{9.2}$$

whereas if $a\overline{p}_2 \geq f'\left(N_{I2}+N_1\right)$, then

$$r = \frac{a\overline{p}_2}{\overline{x}} - 1 \tag{10.1}$$

$$p_2 = \frac{\overline{x}}{a}(1+r) = \overline{p}_2 \tag{10.2}$$

Note that in any case the domestic price p_2 equals the international price $\overline{p}_2$. This is so since in both cases we are using corn as the numeraire, and therefore, we are sterilizing the role of money.

Because of inequalities (1.6), (1.5), and (3.2), there is $\overline{N} > 0$ such that

$$a\overline{p}_2 = f'\left(\overline{N}\right)$$

If $N < \bar{N}$, then the whole population of workers is employed in the production of corn, part of which, $R = f(N) - Nf'(N)$, is exported in order to import foreign cloth; the rate of profits is defined by equation (9.1); an increment of N implies an increment of the corn produced domestically and, therefore, a reduction in the rate of profits.[7] On the contrary, if $N \geq \bar{N}$, then $\bar{N}$ workers are employed in the domestic production of corn, whereas $N - \bar{N}$ workers are employed in the domestic production of cloth. The rate of profits is defined by any of the equations (9.1) and (10.1), which determine the same r; an increment of N has no impact on the rate of profits. Note that $f(\bar{N})$ represents the maximum amount of corn that can profitably be produced domestically at the given international relative price of the two commodities (whether this is for domestic use or for export).

If $\bar{N} < N < \bar{\bar{N}}$, where

$$\bar{\bar{N}} = \bar{N} + \frac{f(\bar{N}) - \bar{N}f'(\bar{N})}{a\bar{p}_2} = \frac{f(\bar{N})}{f'(\bar{N})}, \tag{11}$$

the value of rent is greater than the value of the domestic production of cloth. As a consequence, a share of the domestic production of corn is exported abroad to pay for the import of foreign cloth (the quantity of domestic corn exported is $f(\bar{N}) - \bar{N}f'(\bar{N}) - a(N - \bar{N})\bar{p}_2$).[8] If, instead, $N > \bar{\bar{N}}$, the value of rent is lower than the value of the domestic production of cloth. As a consequence, a share of the domestic production of cloth is exported abroad to pay for the import of foreign corn (the quantity of foreign corn imported is $a(N - \bar{N})\bar{p}_2 - \left[f(\bar{N}) - \bar{N}f'(\bar{N}) \right]$).[9]

The total wage bill, W, and the physical stock of capital, K, are equal to $\bar{x}N$. Total profits, π, may be determined both as $r\bar{x}N$ and as total net output less wages and rents. If $N \leq \bar{N}$, then

$$\pi = N\left(f'(N) - \bar{x} \right),$$

whereas if $N > \bar{N}$,

$$\pi = \bar{N}\left(f'(\bar{N}) - \bar{x} \right) + (a\bar{p}_2 - \bar{x})(N - \bar{N}) = (a\bar{p}_2 - \bar{x})N$$

Interestingly, an increase in a, i.e. an increase in labour productivity in the cloth sector, entails a reduction in $\bar{N}$ and hence a reduction in rent, as noted by Findlay (1974, p. 13) in the statement quoted above.

The same results can be obtained graphically with a modified version of Kaldor's diagram. Taking into account that the marginal cost

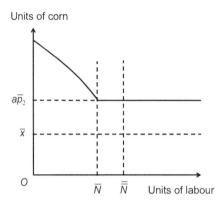

Figure 3.1 Kaldor's diagram for the Ricardian system of a small open economy.

of foreign corn obtained by exporting domestically produced cloth equals $a\bar{p}_2$, the MP curve can be built as in Figure 3.1. If $N < \bar{N}$, then the economy produces only corn and the MP curve of the small open economy coincides with the MP curve of the closed economy in this range. If $N \geq \bar{N}$, then $\bar{N}$ workers are employed in the domestic production of corn and $N - \bar{N}$ in the domestic production of cloth. The MP curve of the small open economy is a horizontal half-line in this range. If $N < \bar{\bar{N}}$, then corn is exported and cloth is imported; if $N > \bar{\bar{N}}$, then cloth is exported and corn is imported; and if $N = \bar{\bar{N}}$, the small open economy behaves like a closed economy since the domestic production of cloth equals the landlords' consumption.

All the formal relations we found among variables are static in the sense that they do not refer to changes over time. *If capitalists invest in their own country*, then equation (9) of Chapter 2 holds and therefore

$$\frac{\dot{N}}{N} = \frac{\dot{K}}{K} = g = \gamma(r), \tag{12}$$

where $\gamma(r)$ is an increasing function such that $\gamma(r_{\min}) = 0$. Thus if $N_t < \bar{N}$ (here the subscript t refers to time), the population grows at a decreasing rate greater than $\gamma((a\bar{p}_2/\overline{xp}_1) - 1) > 0$; an increment of capital results in an increment of N_{1t} and N_{I2t}, whereas $N_{2t} = N_{I1t} = 0$. This is so since only corn is produced domestically and cloth is obtained by importing it in exchange for corn. As soon as $N_t \geq \bar{N}$, the population grows at a constant rate equal to $\gamma((a\bar{p}_2/\overline{xp}_1) - 1) > 0$. That said, the growth rate of the population (and capital) cannot be lower than $\gamma\big((a\bar{p}_2/\overline{x p}_1)-1\big)>0$. Furthermore, if $\bar{N} < N_t < \overline{\overline{N}}$ an increment of capital results in an increment of N_{2t} jointly with an increase of N_{1t} and a decrease of N_{I2t} that leaves the sum $N_{1t} + N_{I2t}$ unchanged, whereas $N_{I1t} = 0$. At $N_t = \bar{N}$ we have $N_{I1t} = N_{I2t} = 0$, and N_{1t} equals what was the sum of $N_{1t} + N_{I2t}$ when $N_t = \bar{N}$. If $N_t > \bar{N}$, N_{1t} is constant and only N_{2t} and N_{I1t} increase, whereas $N_{I2t} = 0$.

3.3 On the production functions and the static gain from trade

Functions (1) and (2) were analysed in Chapter 2 and need no further analysis. Functions (3) and (4) are 'built' from functions (1) and (2) following a procedure that was discussed in Section 3.2. It is worth recalling that this procedure is the same as that illustrated in Section 6 of Chapter 5 of *Theory of Production* (Kurz and Salvadori, 1995). Although land was not considered in that section, the procedure is the same when land in contemplated, as Section 3.2 shows. On the other hand, Kurz and Salvadori (1995) distinguished between tradable and non-tradable commodities, whereas here both corn and cloth are assumed to be tradable. In fact, if only two commodities exist, then either they both are tradable or they both are non-tradable because if only one is tradable and the other is not, then no trade is possible in any case. Moreover, Kurz and Salvadori (1995) also considered that import-export activity may require time and that tariffs and bounties may exist. These aspects are ignored here; but they can easily be studied and are left to the reader, as an exercise.

Chapter 5 of *Theory of Production* is devoted to choice of technique in single production. In order to be able to deal with the case of the small open economy, one simple modification is required: some of the available processes among which producers can choose are import-export processes. These processes are built in the following manner. Let $(\mathbf{a},\mathbf{e}_j,l)$ be a process producing commodity j domestically, and assume that there are no transportation costs either to export commodity j or to import commodity i and that no time is required. Then the process $\big((\bar{p}_i/\bar{p}_j)\mathbf{a},\mathbf{e}_i,(\bar{p}_i/\bar{p}_j)l\big)$ can be interpreted as a process producing commodity i by means of the domestic production of commodity j which is then exported in exchange for the imported commodity i, where $\bar{p}_i$ and $\bar{p}_j$ are the international prices of commodities i and j, respectively, considered as given. If there exist m_i processes to produce the tradable commodity i, with $M = \sum_i m_i$, then opening the economy to trade means including $M - m_i$ processes for each tradable commodity i. Once these processes are included within the set of available processes, the choice of technique determines which commodities will be produced domestically and which are to be imported in exchange for domestically produced commodities. It should be stressed that moving from a closed to an open economy has the same effect as introducing additional production processes, and therefore has an impact that is perfectly analogous to that of technical progress which also involves the introduction of new processes.

In single production, the inclusion of 'new' processes in the set of available processes implies that the *wage frontier* (see Kurz and Salvadori, 1995 for a proper definition) is moved up and to the right.[10] This means a larger wage rate for each rate of profits (i.e. a larger rate of profits for each wage rate). This is what is called the (*static) gain from trade*. It is remarkable that the gain in question is likewise obtained by a country that has an absolute advantage in the production of all commodities, and that even a country which has an absolute disadvantage in the production of all commodities may trade and get a gain from it. Ricardo was conscious of the fact that specialization is not related to absolute advantages, but to *comparative advantages*. He gave a simple example in which two countries, England and Portugal, can produce two commodities: cloth and wine. England exports cloth to Portugal and imports wine, and Portugal exports wine and imports cloth (*Works* I: 134–135). Such a situation happens despite the fact that Portugal has lower real costs in the production of both commodities. Ricardo showed that this exchange comes about because each country has a greater *relative* facility of production in one commodity: wine is *relatively* less expensive to produce than cloth in Portugal, and cloth *relatively* less expensive to produce than wine in England.

Although only ten paragraphs in Chapter 7 of Ricardo's *Principles* concern what are called comparative advantages, standard textbook presentations of the Ricardian theory of international trade place great emphasis on the issue of comparative advantages, which was extensively used by neoclassical economists in their analyses of international trade. It is worth mentioning an episode Samuelson recalled in his Presidential Address to the International Economic Association in 1969, which expresses how much he admired Ricardo and his discovery of comparative advantages. Samuelson and the mathematician Stanislaw Ulam were both members of the Society of Fellows at Harvard (before 1940, when Samuelson become Assistant Professor at MIT), and Ulam used to tease Samuelson by saying "Name one proposition in all of the social sciences which is both true and nontrivial". Samuelson remarked:

This was a test that I always failed. But now, some thirty years later… an appropriate answer occurs to me: The Ricardian theory of comparative advantage… That it is logically true need not be argued before a mathematician; that it is not trivial is attested by the thousands of important and intelligent men who have never been able to grasp the doctrine for themselves or to believe it after it was explained to them.

(Samuelson, 1969, p. 9)

(Comparative advantages are more extensively analysed in the next chapter.)

3.4 On the dynamic gain from trade

As we have seen in Section 3.1, almost all of Ricardo's writings concerning foreign trade (starting from the book *An Essay on Profits* (1815) to the book *On Protection to Agriculture* (1822)) as well as many of his letters to Malthus and Trower focus on the effects that foreign trade has on the domestic rate of capital accumulation and population growth. This issue is called the *dynamic* gain from trade since it relates the extension of the domestic market to the foreign market with the acceleration of economic growth.

The dynamic gain from trade is studied here by comparing the difference between a small open economy in a regime of free international trade and a closed economy with the same population. The two economies are obviously identical if $N = \bar{\bar{N}}$. If $N > \bar{\bar{N}}$, we may easily see that Ricardo was right as concerns the benefits of a free-trade policy: the small open economy enjoys a higher rate of profits and, therefore, a higher rate of economic growth and a lower amount of landlords' rents. This is so since in the closed economy a lower amount of cloth and a larger amount of corn must be produced. But the opposite holds true if $N < \bar{\bar{N}}$. In the closed economy, a larger amount of cloth and a lower amount of corn must be produced; as a consequence, the rate of profits and the rate of economic growth are higher, while rents are lower.

Despite the fact that the intuition is very clear, I will provide a rigorous proof of the statement made above in this section. Let us assume that N is given. In the closed economy, the following equations hold (A is for autarky) for any level of N:

$$R_A = f\left(N_{1A}\right) - N_{1A}f'\left(N_{1A}\right) = aN_{2A}p_{2A}$$

$$N_{1A} + N_{2A} = N$$

$$X_{1A} = f(N_{1A}) = (1+r_A)\bar{x}N_{1A} + f(N_{1A}) - N_{1A}f'(N_{1A})$$

$$X_{2A} = aN_{2A}p_{2A} = (1+r_A)\bar{x}N_{2A}$$

Hence,

$$r_A = \frac{f'(N_{1A})}{\bar{x}} - 1$$

$$p_{2A} = \frac{f'(N_{1A})}{a}$$

$$\frac{f(N_{1A})}{f'(N_{1A})} = N \tag{13}$$

Note that the function on the LHS of equation (13) is an increasing function whose derivative is always greater than 1. In the small open economy, on the other hand, equations concerning prices and the amounts of labour depend on the position of N with respect to $\bar{N}$ and $\bar{\bar{N}}$. The reader will easily calculate that if $N < \bar{N}$, then

$$r_O = \frac{f'(N)}{\bar{x}} - 1,$$

where O stands for open. On the contrary, if $N \geq \bar{N}$, then

$$r_O = \frac{f'(\bar{N})}{\bar{x}} - 1$$

Hence, we merely have to prove that

- $N_{1A} < N$ when $N < \bar{N}$,
- $N_{1A} < \bar{N}$ when $\bar{N} \leq N < \bar{\bar{N}}$,
- $N_{1A} > \bar{N}$ when $N > \bar{\bar{N}}$.

The first statement is obvious. The other two are consequences of equations (11) and (13).

In Section 3.3, there was a gain from trade for all countries. Why is this not so in the analysis of this section? The difference is that in Section 3.3 attention was focused on single production, whereas here we also have land. When land is introduced into the picture, it is of course confirmed that opening the economy to international trade means including a number of processes in the set of available processes. However, when land exists, the inclusion of a number of processes in the set of available processes does not imply that the wage frontier is moved up and to the right. With the opening of the economy to international trade, the distinction between agricultural commodities and industrial commodities no longer holds: a commodity that is agricultural in the closed economy can be produced by importing it in exchange for a commodity that is industrial in the closed economy, and *vice versa*. Hence, it is not impossible that in the open economy scenario, less productive lands are brought into cultivation (whereas they are not under cultivation in the closed economy scenario), or that in the open economy scenario, some lands are cultivated more intensively than is the case in the closed scenario. This means that rent can be higher in the open economy scenario than in the closed one; as a consequence, it may not be the case that a larger wage rate for each rate of profits (i.e. a greater rate of profits for each wage rate) holds in the open economy scenario.

The *positive* dynamic gain from trade was a cornerstone in many of Ricardo's pamphlets and in Chapter VII of the *Principles*. Yet *negative* dynamic gain from trade is never mentioned. Obviously, the same argument that proved that the extension of foreign commerce of corn would *increase* the rate of profit and the rate of growth for England proves also that the extension of foreign commerce of corn would *reduce* the rate of profit and the rate of growth for Poland and for all other countries from which England would import corn. Ricardo acknowledged this fact only partially. In a passage quoted in Section 3.1 and commented also in footnote 4 we read:

> if the commodities obtained at a cheaper rate, by the extension of foreign commerce, or by the improvement of machinery, be exclusively the commodities consumed by the rich, no alteration will take place in the rate of profits.
>
> (*Works* I, p. 132)

As a matter of fact an alteration takes place in the rate of profits: in a corn-exporting country, the rate of profits would be higher in autarky. Indeed, in the above quotation Ricardo's interest is once again devoted to England, as mentioned in Section 3.1.

3.5 Three misleading results

In this section, I consider three results that are correct, given the assumption I have made in this chapter, but which, nevertheless, are misleading. First, let us consider the single production model analysed in Section 3.3. Let $\left(\mathbf{a}, \mathbf{e}_j, l\right)$ be a process producing commodity j domestically, and let $\bar{\mathbf{p}}$ be the given international price vector on the assumption that all commodities are tradable. Then the wage rate which process $\left(\mathbf{a}, \mathbf{e}_j, l\right)$ can pay is

$$w = \frac{\mathbf{e}_j^T \bar{\mathbf{p}} - (1+r)\mathbf{a}^T \bar{\mathbf{p}}}{l}$$

The choice of technique implies that the process(es) which can pay the largest wage rate for a given rate of profits are chosen at that rate of profits. This result suggests that, flukes apart, a small open economy is fully specialized, i.e. it produces and exports a single commodity. This result is a consequence of the fact that the vector $\bar{\mathbf{p}}$ is given at an arbitrary level. Yet this result is clearly misleading: full specialization is quite a rare feature and holds only for very small economies (here 'small' is used in the common sense of the word). As a matter of fact the *given* international price vector is given for the small open economy, but it is determined by the competitive action among all the open economies trading within a *world economy*. As a consequence, the given international price vector is actually given in such a way that for big economies several processes pay the largest wage rate for a given rate of profits.

Another misleading result is, paradoxically, precisely the main result reached in this chapter: a small open economy may grow forever "in wealth and population", to use Ricardo's wording. This is a true result, but it is misleading since international prices *cannot be constant forever*, as can be immediately recognized by considering that each small open economy becomes a cloth-exporting country with population growth, which is clearly impossible. In fact, the *given* international prices are given for the small open economy, but they are determined by the competitive interaction among all the small open economies trading within the *world economy*. As we will see in the following chapters, changes in the international prices are such as to re-establish the stationary state for the world economy in the long run.

In Section 3.2, we assumed that capitalists invest in their own country. But capitalists might invest in countries where the rate of profit is higher than in their own country. In this case, instead of equation (12) a different equation holds and the growth rate could be lower than $\gamma\left(\left(a\bar{p}_2/\bar{x}\right)-1\right) > 0$. Conceivably, one may argue that this is a purely temporary fact since in the long run all rates of profits are uniform among countries. But this is misleading. The 'long run' would presuppose a state in which all countries are cloth exporters! Investments in other countries can be analysed only in the context of a world economy.

3.6 Concluding remarks

The major issue of this chapter is very recent: the main source of the chapter is a paper published online a few months before I delivered the lectures in Graz (see Salvadori and Signorino, 2016). The current presentation is much improved, as the reader will easily recognize. In some sense, the two presentations are a clear proof of the statement put forward in the Preface to this book:

> a book is an excellent opportunity for a scholar who has already published several contributions on an issue to bring together and reorganise his (or her) ideas, to present them in a more general framework, to provide readers with more detailed proofs and to illustrate the argument in terms of numerical examples.

In writing this chapter, I was also prompted to compare developments in a simple model such as that presented here, *including the use of land*, with a much more general model, *excluding the use of land*. The difference is startling: the dynamic gain from trade may be *negative* when land is used. Ricardo himself did not yet recognize this fact, probably on account of his Anglo-centric mindset. But as far as I know, this is not widely recognized even today.

Notes

1 This section is indebted to a paper by Salvadori and Signorino (2017b).
2 By "extension of foreign commerce", we necessarily mean "extension of foreign commerce to further countries" and *not* "extension of import and export volumes".
3 This section owes much to two papers by Salvadori and Signorino (2016, 2017b).
4 Salvadori and Signorino (2015) reconstructed the logic underlying Ricardo's critique in *An Essay on Profits* of Malthus' endorsement of a protectionist food policy. As shown in that paper, Ricardo thought that Great Britain would become a quasi-monopsonist in the international corn market, once it had abandoned a policy of food self-sufficiency.
5 The contrast, made by Ricardo and mentioned in Section 3.1, between "the food and necessaries of the labourer" and "the commodities consumed by the rich" "obtained at a cheaper rate, by the extension of foreign commerce" (*Works* I, p. 132) is better understood by interpreting international

trade as a kind of 'technology': the former is a basic commodity, whereas the latter is a non-basic commodity. As a consequence, a cheaper price of the former increases the rate of profit, whereas a cheaper price of the latter has no effect on the rate of profits. But, as we will see in Section 3.4, this argument does not take enough account of the role of land. Indeed, the contrast noted by Ricardo operates exactly as he maintained only if both "the food and necessaries of the labourer" and "the commodities consumed by the rich" were produced by labour alone.

6 Simple models of this kind are very common in the literature. Readers may consult Kurz and Salvadori (1995), Chapter 3, and especially Sections 3.1 and 3.5.3.

7 The reader can easily calculate that $N_{I1} = N_2 = 0$, N_1 is the solution of the equation

$$Nf'(N) = f(N_1),$$

since N_1 is the amount of labour employed in the production of corn consumed domestically, and $N_{I2} = N - N_1$, since N_{I2} is the amount of labour employed in the production of corn that is exported to obtain the cloth consumed by the landlords.

8 The reader can easily calculate that $N_{I1} = 0$, $N_2 = N - \bar{N}$, since N_2 is the amount of labour not employed in corn production; N_1 is the solution of the equation

$$\bar{N}f'(\bar{N}) + a(N - \bar{N}) = f(N_1),$$

since N_1 is the amount of labour employed in the production of corn consumed by workers and capitalists; and $N_{I2} = \bar{N} - N_1$, since N_{I2} is the amount of labour employed in the production of corn that is exported in order to obtain cloth consumed by the landlords.

9 The reader can easily calculate that $N_{I2} = 0$, $N_1 = \bar{N}$, since all the corn produced is consumed domestically; $N_2 = \left[f(\bar{N}) - \bar{N}f'(\bar{N}) \right]/a$ since N_2 is the amount of labour employed in the production of cloth consumed by the landlords; $N_{I1} = N - \bar{N} - N_2$, since N_{I1} is the amount of labour employed in the production of cloth that is exported in order to obtain corn consumed by the workers and capitalists.

10 However, the small open economy wage frontier may be tangent to the autarkic wage frontier at the rate of profits at which the autarkic prices are proportional to the international prices faced by the small open economy. Obviously at that rate of profits there is no gain from trade.

4 The world economy
Existence of an equilibrium

In Chapter 3, we studied a small open economy model, i.e. a model of an open economy whose inhabitants face *given* international prices. The assumption of *given* and *time-invariant* international prices allowed us to drive home a few analytical results. At the same time, we warned readers that such results may be misleading since they do not hold when this assumption is relaxed and international prices are determined within the model. That is, these results are not robust to alternative model specifications. As a matter of fact, international prices are determined by the trade relationships among trading countries and may vary over time due to the process of capital accumulation and population growth going on within each country. Accordingly, Salvadori and Signorino (2017a) developed a variant of Pasinetti's two-sector model of the Ricardian system in which international trade takes place among several open economies, and international commodity prices are endogenously determined by the trading interplay amongst such countries even if the inhabitants of each country face the international prices as given. This is what is called the *world economy*.

The small open economy model was studied in two different scenarios in Chapter 3: in the case of Pasinetti's two-sector model of the Ricardian system, which is the main topic of this small book, and in the case of an economy in which n commodities are produced with single production processes, and therefore with no use of land. In my view, the comparison between the results obtained in these two scenarios is instructive for readers who are acquainted with the latter scenario, but not with the former. For the same reason, I develop the study of the world economy in the latter scenario in Section 4.1. Readers who are not familiar with such a scenario can skip it with no real loss. Hopefully, others will benefit from reading it.

In the equilibrium of a world economy, the relative 'size' of the various countries matters. In order to better grasp this fact, let us consider a world economy in which there are two open economies with n commodities, all produced by means of single production processes. Let us call them A and B; the relative size of the two countries is such that A is fully specialized in the production of a single commodity, say i, whereas, despite the fact that much of the production of commodity i in A is imported into B in exchange for all other commodities required to satisfy A's needs, domestic demand in B is so large, with respect to the demand in A, that commodity i must be produced domestically also in B. The evident conclusion is that in B at least n production processes are operated, one for each commodity. As a consequence, the international prices of this world economy coincide with the autarkic prices of B, and therefore, no dynamic gain from trade can be obtained by B. This simple example plainly shows that country size matters in a world economy. But the 'size' of each country is changing over time as due to the ongoing process of capital accumulation and population growth. How can we evaluate the relative size of different countries? In this chapter, we consider the size of each country as given in terms of the respective working populations. In Chapter 5, we will consider the dynamics of the world economy in which the size of the various countries becomes a variable magnitude. We will refer to the subject of the analysis provided in this chapter as a world economy in a given moment in time.

In Chapter 3, we saw that Ricardo explicitly used the small open economy assumption and actually obtained a few significant results that may also be partially misleading. What about the world economy? In fact, Ricardo never tried to determine any equilibrium for a world economy nor to obtain any general result concerning it. Nevertheless, he was conscious of the fact that international prices are determined by international competition among trading countries and explicitly considered this problem during the long debates he had with Malthus and other British protectionists. This issue will be considered in Section 4.3.

This chapter may also be useful to introduce a comparison between the analytical apparatus used here and the one that has dominated the theory of international trade for at least 50 years, that is the so-called Heckscher-Ohlin-Samuelson (HOS) model. This is so because in this chapter we consider the world economy in a given moment in time, i.e. we consider the size of each country as given in terms of the respective working populations. This procedure is very similar to the procedure followed by the HOS theorists, who consider distribution as determined by demand for and supply of 'factors of production'.

The structure of the chapter is as follows. In Section 4.1, we study the scenario of an economy in which n commodities are produced with single production processes. A variant of Pasinetti's two-sector model of the Ricardian system for the world economy is presented in Section 4.2. Section 4.3 reconstructs Ricardo's ideas regarding the world economy. Section 4.4 compares it with the HOS theory. Section 4.5 concludes the chapter.

4.1 An excursus: a world economy for single production growing economies[1]

As remarked in Section 3.3, Kurz and Salvadori in their 1995 book on *Theory of Production* dealt with the issue of the small open economy (see Kurz and Salvadori, 1995, pp. 149–150), but not with the issue of the world economy. Subsequently, they investigated the world economy issue in a contribution to the *Festschrift* in honour of Ian Steedman where they constructed a general model in order to analyse international trade (Kurz and Salvadori, 2010). On that occasion, they used a formalism that allowed them to use linear complementarity to determine international prices jointly with the processes that are operated in the existing countries and the intensities of operation of such processes. Moreover, following Steedman (1979a), they assumed that each country has its own uniform rate of profit r_i, the growth rate g is common to all countries, and labour is assumed to be immobile among countries. Since that formalism is mathematically quite demanding, in what follows I propose an easier formalism to reproduce Kurz and Salvadori's (2010) analysis of the world economy in which only two countries exist.

There are n commodities and two countries. Each country has a specific technology defined by the triplet $(\mathbf{A}_j, \mathbf{B}_j, \mathbf{l}_j)$, where $j = 1, 2$, $\mathbf{A}_j$ and $\mathbf{B}_j$ are $m_j \times n$ matrices, and $\mathbf{l}_j$ is a $m_j \times 1$ vector; $\mathbf{A}_j$ is the material input matrix, $\mathbf{l}_j$ is the labour input vector, and $\mathbf{B}_j$ is the output matrix. Commodities are consumed in proportion to vector $\mathbf{d}$. L_j is the working population in country j.

In any long period, equilibrium domestic and international prices $\mathbf{p}$, the wage rates w_j, the intensity of operation vectors $\mathbf{x}_j$, the import vector $\mathbf{y}_j$, and the export vector $\mathbf{z}_j$ must satisfy the inequalities

$$\left[\mathbf{B}_j - \left(1 + r_j\right) \mathbf{A}_j \right] \mathbf{p} \leqq w_j \mathbf{l}_j \tag{1.1}$$

and the equalities

$$\left[\overline{\mathbf{B}}_j - \left(1 + r_j\right) \overline{\mathbf{A}}_j \right] \mathbf{p} = w_j \overline{\mathbf{l}}_j \tag{1.2}$$

$$\mathbf{X}_j^T \left[\overline{\mathbf{B}}_j - (1+g)\overline{\mathbf{A}}_j \right] + \mathbf{y}_j^T = \lambda_j \mathbf{d}^T + \mathbf{z}_j^T \tag{1.3}$$

$$\mathbf{x}_j^T \overline{\mathbf{l}}_j = L_j \tag{1.4}$$

$$\mathbf{d}^T \mathbf{p} = 1 \tag{1.5}$$

$$\mathbf{y}_1 + \mathbf{y}_2 = \mathbf{z}_1 + \mathbf{z}_2 \tag{1.6}$$

where $\left(\overline{\mathbf{A}}_j, \overline{\mathbf{B}}_j, \overline{\mathbf{l}}_j \right)$ is the set of processes that are operated in country j in equilibrium and λ_j are positive scalars. In this section, I provide an algorithm to find the equilibria for all countries if there is an equilibrium for each of the closed economies. Let us call $\overline{w}_j$ the wage rate that holds in country j when it is assumed to be closed to international trade (i.e. $\overline{w}_j$ is the autarkic wage rate in country j).

Step 1. Consider a world economy where the wage rate in country 2 is given at the level $\overline{w}_2$, the autarkic prices of country 2 coincide with the international prices, and country 1 makes the appropriate choice for a small open economy. Call $w_1^{(1)}$ the wage rate that holds in country 1. If $w_1^{(1)} = \overline{w}_1$, then the autarkic prices of the two countries coincide and therefore the unique equilibrium of the world economy has already been found: these economies do not need to trade. If $w_1^{(1)} \neq \overline{w}_1$, then $w_1^{(1)} > \overline{w}_1$.

Step 2. Start from the world economy of Step 1 and consider a fictitious closed economy possessed of all operated processes in country 1 and all operated processes in country 2 except those producing the same commodities produced by the operated processes in country 1. Call it $\left(\overline{\mathbf{A}}^{(2)}, \overline{\mathbf{B}}^{(2)}, \overline{\mathbf{l}}^{(2)} \right)$ and let $\mathbf{x}^{(2)}$ be the solution to the equation

$$\mathbf{x}^T \left[\overline{\mathbf{B}}^{(2)} - (1+g)\overline{\mathbf{A}}^{(2)} \right] = \lambda \mathbf{d}^T,$$

where λ is determined in such a way that

$$\mathbf{x}_2^{(2)T} \overline{\mathbf{l}}_2^{(2)} = L_2,$$

where vectors $\mathbf{x}_j^{(2)}$ and $\mathbf{l}_j^{(2)}$ are obtained by vector $\mathbf{x}^{(2)}$ and $\mathbf{l}^{(2)}$ by substituting the elements corresponding to processes of the country different from j with zero(s). (Below we will follow the same notation also for other vectors.) Then either

$$\mathbf{x}_1^{(2)T} \overline{\mathbf{l}}_1^{(2)} \geq L_1$$

or

$$x_1^{(2)T} \overline{l}_1^{(2)} < L_1$$

In the former case, a solution to system (1) is found: it is enough to reduce the intensity of operation of a process of country 1 and increase the intensity of operation of the process of country 2 producing the same commodity. Let us go on in the assumption that the latter case holds.

Step 3. Start from $\left(\overline{A}^{(2)}, \overline{B}^{(2)}, \overline{I}^{(2)}\right)$ and increase w_2. Hence, w_1 decreases linearly since

$$1 = d^T p = w_1 d^T \left[I + (I+R)\overline{A}^{(2)}\right]^{-1} \overline{l}_1^{(2)} + w_2 d^T \left[I + (I+R)\overline{A}^{(2)}\right]^{-1} \overline{l}_2^{(2)},$$

where R is a diagonal matrix with r_i on the main diagonal when it refers to a process of country i. Vector p is also a linear function of w_2:

$$p = w_1 \left[I + (I+R)\overline{A}^{(2)}\right]^{-1} \overline{l}_1^{(2)} + w_2 \left[I + (I+R)\overline{A}^{(2)}\right]^{-1} \overline{l}_2^{(2)}$$

Go on until another process can be operated. This can be:

(a) a process in country 1 producing a commodity which is produced with processes $\left(\overline{A}^{(2)}, \overline{B}^{(2)}, \overline{I}^{(2)}\right)$ in country 1,
(b) a process in country 1 producing a commodity which is produced with processes $\left(\overline{A}^{(2)}, \overline{B}^{(2)}, \overline{I}^{(2)}\right)$ in country 2,
(c) a process in country 2 producing a commodity which is produced with processes $\left(\overline{A}^{(2)}, \overline{B}^{(2)}, \overline{I}^{(2)}\right)$ in country 1,
(d) a process in country 2 producing a commodity which is produced with processes $\left(\overline{A}^{(2)}, \overline{B}^{(2)}, \overline{I}^{(2)}\right)$ in country 2.

Step 4. Consider a fictitious closed economy possessing the process found in Step 3 and all processes $\left(\overline{A}^{(2)}, \overline{B}^{(2)}, \overline{I}^{(2)}\right)$ except that producing the same commodity produced by the process found in Step 3. Call it $\left(\overline{A}^{(4)}, \overline{B}^{(4)}, \overline{I}^{(4)}\right)$ and then follow the procedure described in Step 2.

The algorithm continues to alternate the analogues of Steps 3 and 4 until step t in which $w_1^{(t)} = \overline{w}_1$ is obtained. Note that the algorithm cannot end in a loop since w_2 is increasing and w_1 is decreasing. Moreover, step t necessarily exists since the set of the available processes is finite. Note that the algorithm allows the definition of a continuous polygonal as in Figure 4.1 in which steps are located along the abscissa and

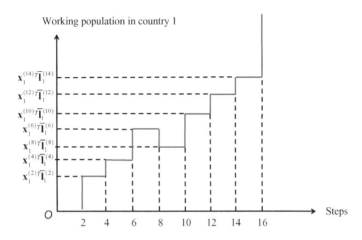

Figure 4.1 The described polygonal.

$\mathbf{x}_1^T \bar{\mathbf{l}}_1$ along the ordinate: the vertical segments are obtained by the use of two processes: the process found in Step $2n+1$ and the process producing the same commodity among the processes $\left(\overline{\mathbf{A}}^{(2n)}, \overline{\mathbf{B}}^{(2n)}, \overline{\mathbf{l}}^{(2n)} \right)$. Such a polygonal can go up (in cases (a), (b), and (d) of the even steps) or down (in case (c) of the even steps), but goes from 0 to infinity, since processes $\left(\overline{\mathbf{A}}^{(t+1)}, \overline{\mathbf{B}}^{(t+1)}, \overline{\mathbf{l}}^{(t+1)} \right)$ coincide with the processes operated in the closed economy. Hence along such a polygonal, the equality

$$ \mathbf{X}_1^T \bar{\mathbf{l}}_1 = L_1 $$

certainly obtains at least once. Note that if the case (c) of the even steps cannot hold, as when there exist only n processes for each country, then the polygonal is non-decreasing and there exists a unique equilibrium. This procedure allows us to determine the processes that are operated in the two countries, vectors $\mathbf{p}$ and $\mathbf{x}_j$, and scalars w_j and λ such that inequalities (1.1); equations (1.2), (1.4), and (1.5); and

$$ \mathbf{x}_1^T \left[\overline{\mathbf{B}}_1 - (1+g)\overline{\mathbf{A}}_1 \right] + \mathbf{x}_2^T \left[\overline{\mathbf{B}}_2 - (1+g)\overline{\mathbf{A}}_2 \right] = \lambda \mathbf{d}^T $$

are satisfied. To conclude, it is necessary to determine vectors $\mathbf{y}_j$ and $\mathbf{z}_j$ and scalars λ_j that satisfy equations (1.3) and (1.6). It is immediately verified that

$$ \lambda_j = \mathbf{x}_j^T \left[\overline{\mathbf{B}}_j - (1+g)\overline{\mathbf{A}}_j \right] \mathbf{p} $$

and

$$\mathbf{y}_j^T - \mathbf{z}_j^T = \lambda_j \mathbf{d}^T - \mathbf{x}_j^T \left[\bar{\mathbf{B}}_j - (1+g)\bar{\mathbf{A}}_j \right]$$

satisfy the desired requirements.

4.2 The Pasinetti-Ricardo world economy model[2]

We assume that there exist n small open countries: A, B, ..., N. The international (and domestic) price of cloth in terms of corn, p_2, is taken as given by any and each trading country. Since Say's Law of Market is assumed to hold, p_2 is determined by the condition that the total amount of rents paid worldwide is able to buy all the cloth produced globally:

$$\sum_J \left[f_J(N_{1J}) - f_J'(N_{1J}) N_{1J} \right] = a p_2 \sum_J N_{2J},$$

where N_{1J} is the amount of labour employed in the domestic production of corn in country J, N_{2J} is the amount of labour employed in the domestic production of cloth in country J, and $J \in \{A, B,..., N\}$.

In this section, following Salvadori and Signorino (2017a), I determine the equilibrium of the world economy when the population in the country J is N_J^* (for all J). The equilibrium of the world economy is determined by means of an algorithm. The starting point is a fictitious state in which $N_J = 0$ for each J; then N_A is increased from 0 to N_A^* keeping $N_J = 0$ for each $J \neq A$; then N_B is increased from 0 to N_B^* keeping $N_A = N_A^*$ and $N_J = 0$ for each $J \neq A, B$; and so on and so forth. All changes in quantity variables are comparative static changes and have no dynamic meaning.

The first stage concerns a closed economy and therefore can be represented as in Figure 2.1 of Chapter 2. We obviously obtain:

$$r_A = \frac{f_A'(N_{1A})}{\bar{x}} - 1 = \frac{a p_2}{\bar{x}} - 1$$

$$N_{2A} = \frac{f_A(N_{1A}) - N_{1A} f_A'(N_{1A})}{a p_2}$$

$$N_A^* = N_{1A} + N_{2A} \tag{2}$$

The first three equations uniquely determine r_A, p_2, N_{2A} as functions of N_{1A}; then the fourth equation determines N_{1A}. The relative price p_2 thus determined is also the international price of cloth in terms of corn at the very beginning of the second stage.

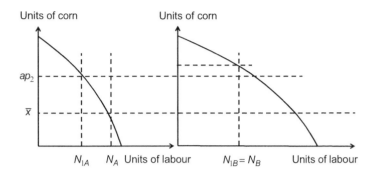

Figure 4.2 Step 2(i).

Let us first represent the other stages assuming that $f'_J(0)$ is the same for each J, that is, that each country has at least one plot of land of the best quality. I will abandon this assumption afterwards. The second stage may be divided into three steps. Any step ends either because the second stage is completed, that is because $N_B = N_B^*$, or because the subsequent step starts.

Step 2(i) can be represented in Figure 4.2, where both countries A and B are present. In the step 2(i), N_B is small, country B produces *only* corn, that is, country B is an agricultural country with no industrial sector. This is so since, in country B, the marginal productivity of labour in corn production at $N_{1B} = N_B$ is larger than the marginal productivity of labour in country A. Therefore, the industrial country A must produce cloth for both countries. Hence, the increase in N_B implies an increase in $N_{2A} = N_A^* - N_{1A}$ and hence a decrease in N_{1A}, which implies an increase in r_A and p_2. Obviously, the rate of profits in the corn-importing country A and the price of the industrial commodity go up, and the industrial country A moves away from the stationary state. Things are different for the corn-exporting country B where

$$r_B = \frac{f'_B(N_B)}{\bar{x}} - 1 > r_A = \frac{f'_A(N_{1A})}{\bar{x}} - 1 = \frac{ap}{\bar{x}} - 1 \qquad (3)$$

and an increase in N_B implies a reduction in r_B. The process goes on until either the second stage is completed ($N_B = N_B^*$) or the two countries attain the same rate of profits ($r_B = r_A$). In algebraic terms, path equilibrium variables are determined by equalities (2), (3), and the following equation:

$$N_{2A} = \frac{f_A(N_{1A}) - N_{1A}f_A'(N_{1A}) + f_B(N_B) - N_B f_B'(N_B)}{ap_2}$$

Consequently,

$$\frac{dN_{1A}}{dN_B} = \frac{f_B''(N_B)N_B}{f_A'(N_{1A}) - N_A f_A''(N_{1A})} < 0$$

Step 2(ii) is represented in Figure 4.3. Now the formerly fully agricultural country B develops a domestic industrial sector, that is, it starts producing cloth at home, and the increase in N_B implies a decrease in $r_B = r_A$ and in p_2. Both countries move towards the stationary state. Note that, while the formerly fully agricultural country B starts industrializing, country A increases its domestic production of corn and reduces its domestic production of cloth. This process goes on until either the second stage is completed ($N_B = N_B^*$) or $N_{1A} = N_A^*$. In the latter case, A has ceased not only to export cloth, but even to produce it domestically, and now produces *only* corn. In other words, the cloth-exporting country A has become a fully agricultural country. In algebraic terms, path equilibrium variables are determined by equation (2) and the following equations:

$$r_B = \frac{f_B'(N_B)}{x} - 1 = r_A = \frac{f_A'(N_{1A})}{x} - 1 = \frac{ap_2}{x} - 1$$

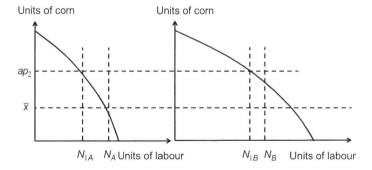

Figure 4.3 Step 2(ii).

$$N_{2A} + N_{2B} = \frac{f_A(N_{1A}) - N_{1A}f'_A(N_{1A}) + f_B(N_{1B}) - N_{1B}f'_B(N_{1B})}{ap_2}$$

$$N_B = N_{1B} + N_{2B} \tag{4}$$

Hence,

$$\frac{dN_{1A}}{dN_B} = \frac{ap_2}{f'_A(N_{1A}) + f'_B(N_{1B})\dfrac{f''_A(N_{1A})}{f''_B(N_{1B})} - f''_A(N_{1A})(N_A + N_B)} > 0$$

$$\frac{dN_{1B}}{dN_B} = \frac{f''_A(N_{1A})}{f''_B(N_{1B})}\frac{dN_{1A}}{dN_B} > 0$$

Step 2(iii) can be represented in Figure 4.4. Now the rate of profits of country A is constant and the increase in N_B implies a decrease in r_B and p_2. The process goes on this way until $N_B = N_B^*$. In algebraic terms, path equilibrium variables are determined by equation (4) and the following equations:

$$r_A = \frac{f'(N_A^*)}{\overline{x}} - 1 > r_B = \frac{f'_B(N_{1B})}{\overline{x}} - 1 = \frac{ap_2}{\overline{x}} - 1$$

$$N_{2B} = \frac{f_A(N_A^*) - N_A^* f'_A(N_A^*) + f_B(N_{1B}) - N_1^{(B)}f'_B(N_{1B})}{ap_2}$$

Hence,

$$\frac{dN_{1B}}{dN_B} = \frac{f'_A(N_{1B})}{f'_A(N_{1B}) - N_{1B}f''_B(N_{1B})} > 0$$

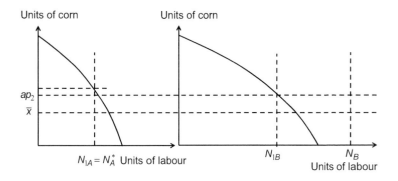

Figure 4.4 Step 2(iii).

At the beginning of the third stage, when country C is introduced, we may have either $r_B \neq r_A$ or $r_B = r_A$. In the former case, the increase in N_C implies an increase in the lowest rate of profits (say r_A) and in p_2, whereas r_C is decreasing and the other rate of profits (say r_B) is constant until $r_B = r_A$ (unless we are stopped by the condition $N_C = N_C^*$). Subsequently (but we start from here if at the beginning of the third stage we have $r_B = r_A$), the increase in N_C implies an increase in $r_B = r_A$ and in p_2 until $r_C = r_B = r_A$ (unless we are stopped by the condition $N_C = N_C^*$). The increase in N_C then implies a decrease in $r_C = r_B = r_A$ and in p_2 until either $N_{1A} = N_A^*$ or $N_{1B} = N_B^*$ (unless we are stopped by the condition $N_C = N_C^*$), say that $N_{1B} = N_B^*$. Subsequently, the increase in N_C implies a decrease in $r_C = r_A$ and in p_2, whereas r_B is constant until $N_{1A} = N_A^*$ (unless we are stopped by the condition $N_C = N_C^*$). Afterwards, the increase in N_C implies a decrease in r_C and p_2, whereas r_A and r_B are constant until $N_C = N_C^*$. And so on and so forth.

Up until now, we have assumed that $f_J'(0)$ is the same for each J. To dispense with such an assumption, assume with no loss of generality that

$$f_A'(0) \leq f_B'(0) \leq \dots \leq f_N'(0)$$

Given such an assumption, the analysis unfolds exactly as before. The only difference is that now, at some stage after the first, country A (and possibly B, C ...) may be in the situation that it does not produce corn domestically and produces only cloth. In such a case, $N_{1A} = 0$, $N_{2A} = N_2^*$, and

$$r_A = \frac{ap_2}{\overline{x}} - 1$$

Let us follow the algorithm in this case. Stage 1 and step 2(i) of stage 2 are the same. The process goes on with step 2(i) until either the second stage is completed ($N_B = N_B^*$) or the two countries attain the same rate of profits ($r_B = r_A$), as before, or until $N_{1A} = 0$ or $N_{2A} = N_2^*$. In the latter case, the algorithm goes on as we have seen before. In the former case, we have step 2(i)bis which is similar to step 2(i), but country A does not produce corn. Figure 4.5 depicts these facts. Like step 2(i), step 2(i)bis goes on until either the second stage is completed ($N_B = N_B^*$) or the two countries attain the same rate of profits ($r_B = r_A$). In this case, step 2(ii)bis starts. It is represented in Figure 4.6. Now the formerly agricultural country B develops a domestic industrial sector and the increase in N_B implies a decrease in $r_B = r_A$ and in p_2. Both countries move toward the stationary state. Note that, while the formerly agricultural country B starts industrializing, the formerly industrial

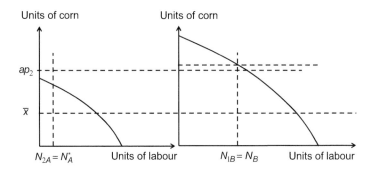

Figure 4.5 Step 2(i)bis.

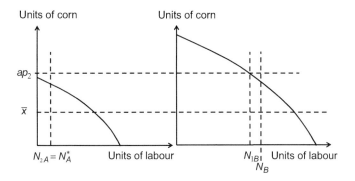

Figure 4.6 Step 2(ii)bis.

country A does not change its production, but the value of the cloth produced in terms of corn goes down. This process goes on until either the second stage is completed ($N_B = N_B^*$) or the marginal product of labour in the corn production of country A equals ap_2. Afterwards, step 2(ii) starts and the algorithm works as we have seen before.

4.3 Ricardo and the world economy[3]

Ricardo devoted Chapter VII of his *Principles* to foreign trade. One of the aims of this chapter is to show that trade among countries may hold even if one country has an absolute advantage in the production of all commodities and that *comparative* advantages are therefore

Table 4.1 Ricardo's four magic numbers

| | Number of men whose labour is required for one year in order to produce a given quantity of | |
	Cloth	*Wine*
In Portugal	90	80
In England	100	120

relevant for determining trade flows and not *absolute* advantages. Ricardo showed this on the basis of a simple example. Let the number of men whose labour is required for one year in order to produce a given quantity of cloth and wine be given as in Table 4.1. Portugal has an absolute advantage in the production of both commodities. Nevertheless, a merchant may get a profit by buying cloth in England and selling it in Portugal in order to buy wine and sell it in England: the merchant has transformed 100 units of labour of Englishmen into 90 units of labour of Portuguese men and finally into 135 units of labour of Englishmen. Similarly, another merchant may get a profit from buying wine in Portugal and selling it in England in order to buy cloth and sell it in Portugal: the merchant has transformed 80 units of labour of Portuguese men into 120 units of labour of Englishmen and finally into 108 units of labour of Portuguese men.

If Portugal and England have non-convertible currencies, this is the obvious business to be done. But what happens if currencies are convertible? In this case if the rate of change of currencies is proportional to labour employed, it is convenient, of course, to sell in England both Portuguese cloth and Portuguese wine. But, Ricardo remarks, this means moving gold from England to Portugal, and therefore, all the prices in Portuguese currency go up and all the prices in English currency go down, and this process goes on until it becomes worth, also in this case, importing wine into England from Portugal and importing cloth into Portugal from England.[4]

All this shows that merchants can obtain a profit by trade. But is this beneficial only for the merchants? The answer is negative. Indeed, "the great profits which are sometimes made by particular merchants in foreign trade" will attract "capital from other employments" such that "the profits of the favoured trade will speedily subside to the general level" (*Works* I: 128–129). This may entail either that the production of wine ceases in England or that the production of cloth ceases in Portugal or both, even if this is not explicitly stated by Ricardo.

As may be immediately recognized, even if Ricardo was able to find the conditions that make it mutually convenient for the two countries involved (England and Portugal) to trade with one another, there is no analysis of the determination of the terms of trade apart from the recognition that prices must change in order to obtain that the profits gained by the merchants in foreign trade are levelled to the general rate of profits.[5] Accordingly, if we look for the concept of the world economy in Chapter VII of the *Principles* we will be disappointed. Yet we encounter the concept of the world economy in other works by Ricardo, viz., in the final section of his last published contribution on corn trade issues, *On Protection to Agriculture* (1822, *Works* IV: 201–270). He wrote:

> Before I conclude, it will be proper to notice an objection which is frequently made against freedom of trade in corn, *viz.*, the dependence in which it would place us for an essential article of subsistence on foreign countries. This objection is founded on the supposition that we should be importers of a considerable portion of the quantity which we annually consume.
>
> (*Works* IV, pp. 264–265)

Ricardo's primary polemical target was the national security argument frequently raised by British protectionists (see de Vivo, 2015) and Malthus. To make the issue of British national security a compelling argument in the public debate between free *versus* restricted international corn trade, its supporters were bound to assume that, in a free-trade regime, Great Britain would *permanently* import a substantial amount of foreign corn during average harvest years. Accordingly, the free-trader Ricardo focused on such an assumption to criticize the national security argument and its food protectionist policy implications. Ricardo's criticism unfolds in two steps. First, he provided arguments to deny that, in a regime of free trade, Great Britain would *permanently* import a substantial amount of foreign corn during average harvest years. Second, he claimed that *even if* Great Britain regularly became a large corn-importing country, its national security would not be endangered by a potential cut of corn exports by foreign agricultural countries:

> In the first place, I differ with those who think that the quantity which we should import would be immense; and, in the second, if it were as large as the objection requires, I can see no danger as likely to arise from it.

With regard to the second part of his criticism, Ricardo basically followed the same line of reasoning already developed seven years before in his *An Essay on Profits* (see Salvadori and Signorino, 2015), which is not relevant to the question in which we are interested here. In what follows, we concentrate on the first step alone.

Ricardo contested the 'substantial importation argument' mainly for the reason that *international prices* would not remain *unchanged* after Great Britain had opened its markets to the importation of corn. Hence, Ricardo is confronted with the need to analyse international prices. He conducted his analysis by means of an insightful blend of empirical elements, drawn from the Report of the 1821 Agricultural Committee, and economic analysis.[6] The empirical element of Ricardo's reasoning concerned the different fertility of the various plots of land in foreign agricultural countries coupled with rising transport costs; the analytical element concerned the dynamics of the international price of corn and the comparative profitability of investment in domestic agriculture *versus* domestic manufactures. He stressed:

> From all the evidence given to the Agricultural Committee, it appears that no very great quantity could be obtained from abroad, *without causing a considerable increase in the remunerating price of corn* in foreign countries. In proportion as the quantity required came from the interior of Poland and Germany, *the cost would be greatly increased by the expenses of land carriage.* To raise a larger supply, too, *those countries would be obliged to have recourse to an inferior quality of land*, and as it is the cost of raising corn on the worst soils in cultivation requiring the heaviest charges, which regulates the price of all the corn of a country, *there could not be a great additional quantity produced, without a rise in the price necessary to remunerate the foreign grower.*
>
> (*Works* IV, p. 265, emphases added)

Ricardo argued that it pays a manufacturing country to import foreign corn whenever the sum of the price of foreign corn (transport costs included) is lower than the price of corn grown at home. In any country, the domestic price of corn is regulated by the cost of production on the marginal, no-rent, plot of land, that is, the least fertile plot of land which it is necessary to cultivate, given the demand for corn. In corn-exporting countries, the overall demand for corn is the sum of domestic *and* foreign demand. Hence, the domestic price of corn in corn-exporting countries, say Germany and Poland, is not independent of manufacturing countries' demand for foreign corn, say Great

Britain. To supply both domestic demand *and* the British demand for foreign corn, German and Polish farmers are obliged to extend the margin of cultivation to plots of land that are *both* increasingly less fertile *and* more distant from German and Polish ports. Accordingly, the more corn Great Britain imports from Germany and Poland, the more the German and Polish production-*cum*-transport costs of corn rise. This is the crucial element that British supporters of food protectionism have neglected and that Ricardo did emphasize: the former have implicitly assumed that the price of foreign corn does not depend on British demand for foreign corn, *as if* foreign corn were produced in a regime of constant costs. By contrast, Ricardo asserted that corn is *universally* produced in a regime of increasing (production-*cum*-transport) costs *both* in Great Britain *and* in Germany and Poland. Hence, according to Ricardo's reasoning, the price of foreign corn is bound to rise in response to a growing British demand for foreign corn. It follows that the comparative profitability of domestic production of corn *versus* foreign corn was not so huge as supporters of restricted international corn trade were inclined to believe:

> In proportion as the price rose abroad, it would become advantageous to cultivate poorer lands at home; and, therefore, there is every probability that, under the freest state of demand, we should not be importers of any very large quantity.
>
> (*Works* IV, p. 265, emphasis added)

As typically is the case with Ricardo, he gives his best in a controversy: in order to counter an argument supported by his opponents, Ricardo produced a remarkable piece of theory. In his pamphlet *On Protection to Agriculture* ([1822] *Works* IV: 201–270), he was able to introduce elements that were not analysed in the *Principles* concerning international prices as determined by countries' competition in the world market.

4.4 Remarks on the HOS theory

HOS theory is named after two Swedish economists, Eli Filip Heckscher (1919) and Bertil Gotthard Ohlin (1933), and Nobel laureate Paul Anthony Samuelson (1948, 1949). In this section, my first task is to recall all the assumptions employed by Samuelson (1949) and make it clear how they differ from those adopted in the model presented in Section 4.2.

Assumption 1: "There are but two countries".

Assumption 2: "They produce but two commodities, food and clothing".

Assumption 3: "Each commodity is produced with two factors of production, land and labour" and returns to scale are constant.

Assumption 4: "The law of diminishing marginal productivity holds".

Assumption 5: Food is relatively land-intensive while clothing is relatively labour-intensive.

Assumption 6: "Land and labour are assumed to be qualitatively identical inputs in the two countries and the technological production functions are assumed to be the same in the two countries".

Assumption 7: "All commodities move perfectly freely in international trade". "No factors of production can move between the countries".

Assumption 8: "Something is being produced in both countries of both commodities with both factors of production".

Before comparing Samuelson's assumptions and the assumptions entertained here, I want to stress that Samuelson is very accurate by calling the factors endowed by the two countries: labour and land (but he failed to be so accurate in Section 5 of his essay). Unlike capital, labour and land are two 'original' factors of production, that is, they cannot be (re)produced in a capitalistic way. Other, less accurate, formulations of HOS theory take the given endowment of a country to consist of labour and 'capital' without taking into consideration that capital consists, in general, of the payments advanced by the capitalists and that material capital consists of produced means of production and therefore they need to be (re)produced. The consequences of this unfortunate attempt to (mis)apply the results obtained by Samuelson within models with labour and land only to models with labour and capital have been dealt with in a critical debate of such literature that started in the 1970s with Parrinello, Steedman, Metcalfe, and Mainwaring (see Steedman, 1979b), and will not be explored here.

In Section 4.2, Assumption 1 does not need to hold; for the sake of comparison, we consider the cases in which it holds. Assumptions 2 and 7 also hold in the model here presented in Section 4.2: the only (irrelevant) difference is that we call corn what Samuelson called food. However, I stress that in Section 4.2 Assumption 7 holds only for the purposes of the analysis of this chapter and will be removed in the next chapter. A small difference holds with respect to Assumption 3: here cloth is produced by labour alone, whereas Samuelson's Assumption

3 allows that cloth might also be produced by labour and land. This difference implies another small difference with respect to Assumption 4 (in the analytical apparatus of Section 4.2 it applies to corn, but not to cloth) and Assumption 5 (in Section 4.2 it holds, but is not an assumption, being a consequence of the fact that cloth is produced without using land). Assumption 6 requires more attention. In the analytical apparatus of Section 4.2, it is true that "Land and labour are assumed to be qualitatively identical inputs in the two countries", but we allow different qualities of land and even if the same qualities may be present in both countries they do not need to be present in the same proportions. The consequence is that even if the two countries share the same technology, that is the same processes of production – as assumed here – they do *not* share the same production functions of corn. This point has been extensively treated in Section 1.2. Assumption 8 is not adopted here, but nevertheless there are cases in which it holds.

Samuelson (1949) proves that under Assumptions 1–8 "real factor prices must be exactly the same in both countries". This result, generally referred to as the "Factor–price equalization theorem", is also obtained in Section 4.2 in those cases in which all countries produce both corn and cloth, despite the fact that Assumption 6 does not hold in the form stated by Samuelson and even when Assumption 1 does not hold. This should also clarify the role of Assumption 8 in HOS theory. Samuelson is very conscious of this fact and explores this condition in Section 6 of his essay whose *incipit* is "If complete specialisation takes place in one country, then our hypothesis is not fulfilled and the conclusion does not follow". In the model here presented if a country produces only corn, it may experience a higher rate of profit than the rate of profit holding in countries producing both corn and cloth (see Figures 4.2 and 4.4), whereas if a country produces only cloth, it may experience a lower rate of profit than the rate of profit holding in a country producing only corn (see Figure 4.5) or it experiences the same rate of profit than the rate of profit holding in a country producing both corn and cloth (see Figure 4.6). The asymmetric behaviour of corn and cloth is of course a consequence of the fact that cloth is produced by labour alone.

The Factor–price equalization theorem is one of the four propositions that are considered the core of HOS theory. The others are referred to as "Heckscher-Ohlin theorem", "Rybczynski theorem", "Stolper-Samuelson theorem". Let us recall them and show how they are connected with the results presented in this book.

The Heckscher-Ohlin theorem asserts that exports of the land-abundant country consist of the land-intensive commodity, and the labour-abundant country imports such a commodity, exporting the labour-intensive commodity in return. I will not discuss here how these concepts are defined. With regard to the results of Section 4.2, it is clear that the statement is fulfilled. Indeed when along the algorithm investigated in Section 4.2 the working population increases in country B, we have seen that country B produces only corn when the size of the working population is very small; then, after a threshold, country B starts the production of cloth, but it continues to import corn; then, after another threshold, country B stops importing corn and starts exporting cloth. Moreover, prior to the second-mentioned threshold, country A produces and exports cloth whereas it imports cloth afterwards. Further, there may exist another threshold after which country A can even produce only cloth (see Figure 4.5).

However, let us direct our attention to the fact that in the next chapter we will discuss an example in which the working population increases *proportionally* in both countries and we obtain a trade pattern reversal. Indeed, we could also obtain more than one trade pattern reversal as a consequence of a proportional increase of the working population. This is of course not contemplated by the Heckscher-Ohlin theorem. As we will see, the collapse of the theorem is a consequence of the fact that the two countries do not share the same production functions even if they share the same technology, that is, that not only intensive rent, but also extensive rent is possible.

The Rybczynski theorem asserts that when the amount of one factor of production increases, the production of the commodity that uses that production factor intensively increases relative to the increase in the factor of production. In the model of Section 4.2, this clearly holds when the country in which labour increases produces both commodities. On the contrary, in the very early stage of the labour increasing in country B, the effect is to increase the production of corn in country B. Therefore in country B, rents are increased and the rate of profits is reduced even if this implies an increase of cloth production in country A and a rise in the international price of cloth in terms of corn and the rate of profits and a reduction of rents in country A. Once more the role of Samuelson's Assumption 8 is relevant.

The Stolper-Samuelson theorem asserts that changes in commodity relative prices drive the relative prices of the factors used to produce them. This theorem concerns the small open economy. If we consider Figure 3.1, we can easily check that an increment of $\bar{p}_2$ implies a reduction of $\bar{N}$ and $\bar{\bar{N}}$. Once more the theorem holds when both commodities are produced: rents are reduced and the rate of profits is increased as a consequence of an increment of $\bar{p}_2$. But it may not hold if only corn is produced.

4.5 Concluding remarks

The main source of the chapter is a paper published online a few months after the lectures (see Salvadori and Signorino, 2017a). In writing the chapter, I compared once again what happens in a simple model like the one presented here *with the use of land* with a model with many commodities *without the use of land*. Moreover, I explored two further issues. The first concerns Ricardo's writings: did Ricardo recognize the need for and the role of the concept of a world economy? The answer is in the affirmative, despite the fact that the concept cannot be found in his *Principles*, but only in a pamphlet, where the concept was introduced to criticize his opponents. The second concerns the HOS theory and how the results presented here compare with those supported by this theory. It turned out that there are two assumptions that are very important in deriving the different results. But still more important differences will be put forward in Chapter 5 where the world economy is analysed and not just its situation at a given moment in time, but its development over time. The criticism that emerges is not related to capital, since in the models analysed in this book physical capital, that is, produced means of production, is not dealt with: it is, therefore, different from the criticism developed in the 1970s (see Steedman, 1979b). The latter strand of literature dealt with trade pattern reversals in comparative static analyses connected to changes in income distribution in economies with one (labour) or two (labour and land of uniform quality) primary factors. Trade pattern reversals are there related to the existence of produced means of production and their revaluation when distribution changes. In contrast, the trade pattern reversal we will see in Chapter 5 takes place along a path of capital accumulation and population growth and is related to the existence of extensive rent.

Notes

1 This section is indebted to a paper by Kurz and Salvadori (2010). Yoshinori Shiozawa (2017) provided a much more complete and detailed analysis.
2 This section owes much to two papers by Salvadori and Signorino (2017a, 2017b).
3 This section is indebted to a paper by Freni, Salvadori and Signorino (2019a).
4 Heinz Kurz (2017) provided an illuminating "plain man's guide" to understanding Ricardo's principle of comparative advantage. I also benefited from reading the English translation of an article by K. Yukizawa (1974). I thank Susumu Takenaga for sending me this translation and I hope that it will be soon available in print.

5 Ricardo only tells us that the terms of trade are not determined like they are within the same country:

> The quantity of wine which [Portugal] shall give in exchange for the cloth of England, is not determined by the respective quantities of labour devoted to the production of each, as it would be, if both commodities were manufactured in England, or both in Portugal.
>
> (Works, I: 134–135)

6 The Report of the 1821 Agricultural Committee was presented to the House of Commons on 1 April 1822; while Ricardo's pamphlet was published 17 days later.

5   The world economy
The dynamics

In Chapter 4, I introduced the world economy model, i.e. a model in which international trade takes place among several small open economies and international commodity prices are endogenously determined by the interplay amongst trading countries. However, in that chapter the scope of the analysis was limited to a *given moment in time* and therefore the size of each country was considered as given in terms of the respective working populations. By contrast, this chapter is devoted to the dynamics of the world economy and therefore the sizes of the various countries are considered as time-dependent magnitudes. The aim is to determine exactly how the accumulation of capital is realized, and therefore how working populations grow.

A formal presentation of the dynamic properties of the world economy is certainly too complex to be dealt with in this small book. What I have sought to do in this chapter is to provide a general discussion of the issue and develop two numerical examples. The examples (the first of which was originally produced by Freni, Salvadori, and Signorino, 2019b) will also be able to clarify some implications of the Ricardian theory of differential extensive rent in a free-trade regime. Indeed, accumulation of capital may imply that a country that feeds its own population mainly by importing foreign food and paying for food imports by exporting industrial commodities in a stage of worldwide capital accumulation may, at a subsequent stage, completely reverse the pattern of its imports and exports. Similarly, it is also possible that a country at a given moment in time is a cloth exporter, but subsequently becomes specialized in corn production. It is even possible that a country is specialized in the production of cloth at one stage, but at another specializes in the production of corn.

It may be useful to give here the intuition followed by Giuseppe Freni, Rodolfo Signorino, and myself. Assume that there are only two trading countries, A and B; two qualities of land, high and low; and two commodities, one agricultural (corn) and one industrial (cloth). Both countries have a large territory, but *A* is endowed with a small quantity of high-quality land and a large quantity of low-quality land, while the opposite situation holds in *B*. When the level of capital accumulated worldwide is low, it is worthwhile for *A* to cultivate only its high-quality plots of land and feed its population mainly by importing corn from *B*. Corn imports from *B* are obviously paid by exports of cloth to *B*. Accordingly, at first, *A* is a typical industrial and corn-importing country, while *B* is a typical agricultural and cloth-importing country. As worldwide capital accumulation continues and both countries' populations increase, a point in time arrives when, in order to feed the world population, the cultivation of low-quality land is required. When this happens, world production of corn increases more rapidly in the country endowed with the larger quantity of low-quality land, i.e. *A*. This effect may be so strong that *A* may even become a corn-exporting country. Obviously, such a result does not obtain if the two qualities of land are uniformly distributed between the two trading countries, i.e. if *A* and *B* have the same ratio of high- to low-quality land. Further, if *A* is endowed only with a large quantity of low-quality land and no high-quality land at all, then when the level of worldwide capital accumulation is still very low, *A* is specialized in cloth production. Nevertheless, when the level of worldwide capital accumulation is very high, *A* could well be specialized in corn production.

It needs to be stressed that a scenario in which worldwide capital accumulation reverses the pattern of international specialization among trading countries is incompatible with the interpretation of the open Ricardo-Pasinetti model as a variant of the textbook 2×2×2 Heckscher-Ohlin model. Findlay (1974) advanced such an interpretation, stating that in the Ricardian system

> the pattern of specialization would depend upon differences in any or all of the following: the technology for producing the two commodities, the natural wage-rate, the composition of landlord demand and the proportions of labour (and hence circulating capital) to land

and that "if all the other differences except the last were excluded by assumption the Ricardo-Pasinetti system would also lead to a factor proportions theory of comparative advantage" (Findlay, 1974, p. 11). The implicit assumption made by Findlay (1974) is that two countries that share *the same technology* have *the same production functions*. But we have seen that this need not be true. The examples developed in this chapter show once again that differences in the availability of land qualities mimic differences in technology and, therefore, one cannot expect the basic propositions of the textbook Heckscher-Ohlin model to continue to hold unaltered. Indeed, for the analogous two-sector dynamic Heckscher-Ohlin model, the long-run direction of trade is determined by the difference in the factor proportions prevailing at the time the two countries adopt free trade. Accordingly, a country that initially imports a given commodity can never become a country that exports it (see, for example, Chen, 1992; Bajona and Kehoe, 2010). When more than one quality of land is taken into consideration, this result ceases to hold since two countries sharing the same technology may have different production functions.

This chapter highlights the fact that capital accumulation may reverse the pattern of international specialization among trading countries. Did Ricardo ever recognize this fact? It would seem not. However, Ricardo mentions a case of reversal of the pattern of international specialization among trading countries in Chapter VII of the *Principles*. This fact cannot remain undiscussed here.

The structure of the chapter is as follows. Section 5.1 provides a general discussion concerning the dynamics of a world economy. Section 5.2 develops the data relative to one of the above-mentioned examples. Sections 5.3 and 5.4 develop the analysis of the dynamics of capital and working populations within the boundaries of the proposed example without paying attention to the export/import aspects of the example. These issues are studied in Section 5.5. Section 5.6 develops a different example with even stronger differences with respect to the basic propositions of the textbook Heckscher-Ohlin model. Section 5.7 discuss a case of reversal of the pattern of international specialization among trading countries mentioned by Ricardo in Chapter VII of the *Principles*. Finally, Section 5.8 concludes the chapter.

5.1 A general discussion concerning the dynamics of a world economy

The issue of the economy's dynamics has been considered since Chapter 1, where the rate of growth was treated as positive whenever the rate of profits is above a given minimum value. This assumption was formalized in Chapter 2, where, following Pasinetti (1960), the rate of growth-rate of profits relationship was stated as

$$g = \gamma(r), \tag{1}$$

where $\gamma(r)$ is an increasing function such that $\gamma(r_{min}) = 0$. For the sake of simplicity $r_{min} = 0$ was also posited, so that if $r > 0$, then g is positive and capital is increasing over time as are working population and workers employed in agriculture. As a consequence, r and p_2 decline over time until $r = 0$, $ap_2 = \bar{x}$, and the growth rate is nought: the stationary state is obtained (see Figure 2.2). The same procedure was followed for a small open economy in Chapter 3, on the assumption that capitalists invest only in their own country. This allowed us to prove that in the small open economy set-up the growth rate of population (and capital) cannot be lower than $\gamma\left(\left(a\bar{p}_2/\bar{x}\right)-1\right) > 0$. In the same chapter, however, I remarked that despite the fact that capitalists might be tempted to move their capital abroad if the foreign rate of profits is higher than the domestic rate, the issue of international capital movements cannot be analysed in the context of the small open economy: investments in foreign countries can be analysed only in the context of a world economy. This is what I do here. But let us first recall what we learned in Chapter 4.

In the world economy scenario, there are as many rates of profits as there are countries. If the rates of profits are uniform among countries, that is, if all countries produce some cloth,[1] then an increase in any country's working population results in a fall in the common rate of profits and in the price of the industrial commodity. Further, if function (1) is common to all countries, capital and population grow proportionally in all countries and all countries move toward the stationary state. Things are different in the case in which the rates of profits differ among countries, that is, when not all countries produce cloth. In this case, there is a set of countries that produce cloth (no matter whether or not they export it) and a set of countries that do not produce cloth. All countries that produce cloth exhibit the same rate of profits, which is also lower than or equal to the rate of profits of each of the other countries.

Let a country produce only corn and experience a higher rate of profits than that attained both in countries producing both corn and cloth (see Figures 4.2 and 4.4) and in countries producing only cloth (see Figure 4.6). An increment of the working population in any country producing only corn:

  i) reduces the rate of profits in this country,
 ii) increases the rate of profits in countries producing (either both corn and cloth or only) cloth,
iii) increases the international price of cloth,
 iv) leaves unchanged the rate of profits in all other countries producing only corn (provided that the rate of profits in countries producing cloth remains below the rate of profits in these countries).

By contrast, an increase in the working population in any country producing cloth:

i)   reduces the rate of profits in all countries producing cloth,
ii) reduces the international price of cloth,
iii) leaves unchanged the rate of profits in all countries producing only corn.

In this chapter, I will not formalize the equivalent of function (1) for the world economy. Two polar cases are possible. In the first, capitalists invest only in countries with the highest rate of profits. In this case, the international price of cloth and the rate of profits in the countries with the lowest rate of profits go up. Hence, the countries with the lowest rate of profits move away from the stationary state. Correspondingly, the rate of profits in the countries with the highest rate of profits goes down and the countries with the highest rate of profits move toward the stationary state. In all the other countries, the rates of profits are unchanged and so are rents, even if landlords may buy less cloth with their rents. In the second case, capitalists invest only in their own country and function (1) applies. In this case, in all countries capital and working populations increase, but they increase more in countries with the highest rate of profits. One way or the other, the rate of profits tends to level out among trading countries. As soon as this happens, an increase in capital and working population in any country pushes all countries toward the stationary state.

Between these two polar cases, we may assume that the growth rate of capital and working population in a given country is a function of the rate of profits in all countries. In short, we may assume that capital investment is home-biased, provided that of course the spread between the foreign and the domestic rate of profits is below a given threshold. Ricardo himself clearly acknowledged that the two polar cases sketched above are unrealistic:

> If the profits of capital employed in Yorkshire, should exceed those of capital employed in London, capital would speedily move from London to Yorkshire, and an equality of profits would be effected; but if in consequence of the diminished rate of production in the lands of England, from the increase of capital and population, wages should rise, and profits fall, it would not follow that capital and population would necessarily move from England to Holland, or Spain, or Russia, where profits might be higher.
>
> (*Works* I, p. 134)

Ricardo explained capitalists' home bias both on subjective grounds (family ties) and on objective grounds (expensive monitoring, costs associated with managing capital in an unknown juridical and security environment, etc.):

> Experience ... shews, that the fancied or real insecurity of capital, when not under the immediate control of its owner, together with the natural disinclination which every man has to quit the country of his birth and connexions, and intrust himself with all his habits fixed, to a strange government and new laws, check the emigration of capital. These feelings, which I should be sorry to see weakened, induce most men of property to be satisfied with a low rate of profits in their own country, rather than seek a more advantageous employment for their wealth in foreign nations.
>
> (*Works* I, pp. 136–137)

Yet, in any case, whatever assumption we make concerning international capital movements, the stationary state is the unavoidable conclusion of the story. Yet though the stationary state is the unavoidable destiny of the world economy in the given circumstances, the path each country actually follows toward the stationary state is quite different from that followed in the closed economy scenario investigated in Chapter 2. Indeed, in that scenario the path is monotonic in the sense that the rate of profits decreases through the whole period going from the initial state to the stationary state. By contrast, in the world economy scenario this path needs to be monotonic *if and only if* all countries have exactly the same rate of profits and therefore all countries produce cloth (even if some of them export it and others import it). On the contrary, if some countries do not produce cloth – and have a higher rate of profits – any investment in these countries entertains an increase in their population, which leads to an increase in the rate of profits in the countries with the lowest rate of profits, that is, the cloth-producing countries.

5.2 An example

Let us consider a world economy in which there are two countries, *A* and *B*. Technology is the same in both countries. There are two different qualities of land: high quality and low quality (*h* and *l*). For the sake of simplicity, let us assume that (i) country *A* has both qualities of land, whereas country *B* has only high-quality land and (ii) the surface area of high-quality land is the same in both countries. It must be stressed that what really matters is the fact that the ratio of high- to low-quality land in country *A* is different from the ratio of high- to low-quality land in country *B*. The results we will obtain crucially depend on the different high- to low-quality land ratio assumption and on nothing else.

In the light of the above assumptions on technology and each country's land endowment, it is possible to formalize the production functions for the two commodities as follows. As regards cloth production, the two production functions in the two countries are:

$$X_{2A} = aN_{A2}$$
$$X_{2B} = aN_{B2}$$

where X_{2J} is the quantity of cloth produced in country *J* (*J* = *A, B*) and N_{J2} is the number of workers employed in cloth production in country *J*. With regard to corn production, we first note that a description of technology in terms of production processes as that adopted in Chapter 1 would certainly be preferable, but it would also be very cumbersome to manage. It is convenient, instead, to consider that on each quality of land we have a production function described by a simple formula (such as a Cobb-Douglas or a parabola) and combine them. This means that intensive rent is always present, whereas extensive rent appears only when a new quality of land is cultivated. The two production functions for corn in the two countries are:

$$X_{1A}(N_{A1}) = \max \left\{ \begin{array}{l} N_{A1h}^m + \alpha N_{A1l} - \beta N_{A1l}^2 : \\ N_{A1h} + N_{A1l} = N_{A1}, N_{A1h} \geq 0, N_{A1l} \geq 0 \end{array} \right\}$$
$$X_{1B}(N_{B1}) = N_{B1}^m$$

where X_{1J} is the quantity of corn produced in country *J* (*J* = *A, B*); N_{J1} is the number of workers employed in the corn production in country *J*; $0 < m < 1$, $\alpha > 0$, $\beta > 0$ are constants and the inequalities result from diminishing returns in corn production. Note that necessarily $N_{A1l} \leq \alpha / 2\beta$. The production function for corn in country *A* can be written, in a more explicit form, as

$$X_{1A}(N_{A1}) = \left\{ \begin{array}{ll} N_{A1}^m & \text{if } 0 \leq N_{A1} \leq \left(\dfrac{\alpha}{m}\right)^{\frac{1}{m-1}} \\ \left[g(N_{A1})\right]^m + & \\ \alpha\left[N_{A1} - g(N_{A1})\right] - & \text{if } N_{A1} \geq \left(\dfrac{\alpha}{m}\right)^{\frac{1}{m-1}} \\ \beta\left[N_{A1} - g(N_{A1})\right]^2 & \end{array} \right.$$

where $N_{A1h} = g(N_{A1})$ is equivalent to the equation

$$\frac{\alpha - mN_{A1h}^{m-1}}{2\beta} + N_{A1h} = N_{A1}$$

Since the left-hand side of this equation is an increasing function in N_{A1h} with a derivative larger than 1, function $g(N_{A1})$ is well defined, increasing, and its derivative is lower than 1.

The above equations conclude the description of the technology in the two countries. The following sections are devoted to an analysis of the example.

5.3 The phase space of the world economy

In this section, I partition the space (N_B, N_A) in order to distinguish the portions of the space in which the dynamics of populations and capitals of the two countries can be characterized. That is, I will define the phase space of the dynamics of capitals and populations of the world economy. More precisely, in this section, I will define only the different portions of the phase space, but they will be determined in an appendix, Section 5.A1. Figure 5.1 represents the phase space. On the horizontal axis, there is labour in country B which, when multiplied by $\bar{x}$, gives the amount of (corn-)capital in country B. On the vertical axis, there is labour in country A which, when multiplied by $\bar{x}$, gives the amount of (corn-)capital in country A. Both countries produce corn since both countries have plots of land of the best quality: only a country that does not have plots of land of the best quality may be specialized in cloth production when the marginal productivity of labour in the corn sector is lower than ap_2, even if the population employed in corn production is nought. By contrast, it may be the case that only one country produces cloth.

Even though both countries share the same agricultural technology, their production functions for corn turn out to be different because their high- to low-quality land ratio is different. It must be stressed that if only high-quality land is employed in each country, that is, if low-quality land is left idle in country A, then the production functions for corn are the same in both countries. This is so if $0 \le N_{A1} \le (m/\alpha)^{\frac{1}{1-m}}$. By contrast, if $N_{A1} > (m/\alpha)^{\frac{1}{1-m}}$, then the low-quality land is cultivated in country A and the production functions for corn are inevitably different. Hence, it is of crucial importance to determine the portion of the space (N_B, N_A) in which the two countries share the same production functions. This will be done by determining the locus

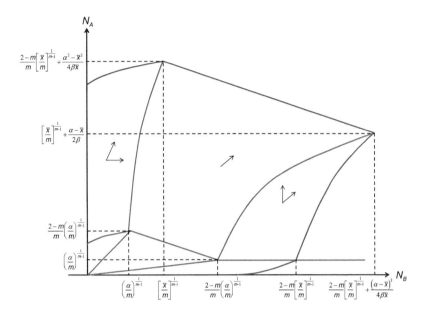

Figure 5.1 The phase space when $m = 1/2$, $\alpha = 2$, $\beta = 1/2$

in which $N_{A1} = N_{A1h} = (m/\alpha)^{\frac{1}{1-m}}$. Below this locus, low-quality land is not cultivated in country A, whereas above this locus it is cultivated in country A. Along the locus $\bar{x}(1+r_A) = mN_{A1}^{m-1}$, and this value equals ap_2 if cloth is produced in country A; otherwise, it may be larger than ap_2. The locus is represented by a purple line in Figure 5.1 and I will refer to it as the purple line.

Some points of the space (N_B, N_A) cannot be reached (on the assumption that the initial conditions never require negative investments). Since the growth rate of population of a country may be nought in some points of the space (N_B, N_A), the population of that country cannot grow enough to reach some other points. In particular, the world economy cannot reach all the points of the space (N_B, N_A) that are:

- above and on the right of the locus in which the rate of profits is nought in both countries;
- above the locus in which the rate of profits of country A is nought and the rate of profits of country B is positive;
- on the right of the locus in which the rate of profits of country B is nought and the rate of profits in country A is positive.

These loci are all represented as a brown line in Figure 5.1 and I will refer to their set as the brown line. Along this line the rate of profits in at least one country equals zero and therefore $ap_2 = \bar{x}$, and this value is not lower than the marginal productivity of labour in corn production and is equal to it in any country in which cloth is produced.

The portion of space (N_B, N_A) bounded by the brown line is the relevant part of the space, and we ignore what happens beyond it. This portion can be divided into three parts. In the central part both countries produce cloth, and therefore, they share the same rate of profits and the same growth rate. Consequently, within this part N_A and N_B grow in proportion, and therefore, any trajectory of populations and capitals in this area lies along a straight line passing through the origin. Note that along these trajectories the common rate of profits is decreasing. This portion of the phase space will be referred to as the *no specialization area*.

In the part to the right of the no specialization area, cloth is produced only in country B, whereas country A is specialized in corn production. This portion of the phase space will be referred to as the *A specialized area*. In the corn-specialized country, the rate of profits and the rate of growth are higher than in country B. As a consequence, any trajectory of populations and capitals in this area is along a curve whose tangent in each point is steeper than the slope of the straight line passing from the point in which the tangent is calculated and the origin. Thus, both the first and the second derivatives are positive. Note that along these trajectories the rate of profits in country A is decreasing, whereas the rate of profits in country B may be increasing and is certainly increasing when this line is almost vertical. By the way, in the no-home bias case, that we have excluded, in which capitalists invest only in the country with the highest rate of profits, the mentioned curve would be a vertical straight line. In Figure 5.1, the A specialized area is separated from the no specialization area by a red line. Along the red line both countries share the same rate of profits, but only country B produces cloth.

The part to the left of the no specialization area will be referred to as the *B specialized area* since cloth is produced only in country A. Since the rate of profits and the rate of growth are higher in country B, any trajectory of populations and capitals in this area is along a curve whose tangent in each point is less deep than the slope of the straight line passing from the point in which the tangent is calculated and the origin. Thus, the first derivative is positive, whereas the second derivative is negative. Note that along these trajectories the rate of profits in country B is decreasing, whereas the rate of profits in country A

may be increasing and is certainly increasing when this line is almost horizontal. By the way, in the no-home bias case, in which capitalists invest only in the country with the highest rate of profits, the above-mentioned line would be horizontal. In Figure 5.1, the *B* specialized area is separated from the no specialization area by a blue line. Along the blue line both countries share the same rate of profits, but only country *A* produces cloth.

5.4 Trajectories of the world economy

Properties of trajectories *within* the three areas separated by the blue and the red lines have been illustrated with the help of Figure 5.1. In this section, I make use of Figure 5.2 to illustrate the dynamic movements from one area to the others. In Figure 5.2, points *A* and *B* are introduced. They are the points on the blue line and on the red line, respectively, where these lines are tangent to a straight line passing through the origin.

Because of the properties of the trajectories within the no specialization area, it is easy to recognize that any trajectory of a world economy can cross the blue line from the *B* specialized area to the no specialization area only below point *A*. On the contrary, any trajectory of a world economy can cross the blue line from the no specialization area to the *B* specialized area only above point *A*. Further, it may be the case that a trajectory of a world economy can be characterized by the fact that country *B* is specialized in corn production at time t, then is not specialized at time t', and then is specialized again at time t'', with $t < t' < t''$. This happens when its trajectory lies, in the no specialization area, on a straight line passing through the origin and cutting the blue line twice.

Similarly, any trajectory of a world economy can cross the red line from the *A* specialized area to the no specialization area either above point *B* or below the purple line, whereas any trajectory of a world economy can cross the red line from the no specialization area to the *A* specialized area only below point *A* and above the purple line. Moreover, it may be the case that a trajectory of a world economy can be characterized by the fact that country *A* is not specialized at time t, then is specialized in corn production at time t', and then is not specialized again at time t'', with $t < t' < t''$. This happens when its trajectory lies, in the *no specialization area*, on two different straight lines going through the origin and cutting the red line below and above point *B*, respectively.

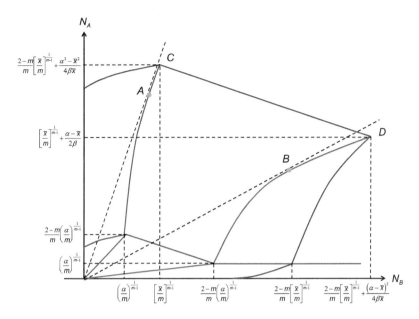

Figure 5.2 Dynamics through the areas.

Figure 5.2 can also be used to point out that any trajectory of a world economy terminates on a point of the segment *CD*. Along this segment the rate of profits is zero in both countries and therefore also the rate of growth is zero. In any other point of the relevant part of the phase space, at least one country has a positive rate of profits and therefore a positive rate of growth. In particular, any trajectory joining the brown line at a point to the left of point *C* continues necessarily along the brown line toward point *C*. Similarly, any trajectory joining the brown line at a point below point *D* continues necessarily along the brown line toward point *D*. This is so since the growth rate in the specialized country is positive. However, further investments reduce the rate of profits together with the rate of growth in this country.

5.5 The patterns of trade

This section is devoted to rendering explicit the patterns of trade of the example presented and analysed in Sections 5.2–5.4. To that end we need to partition the *no specialization area*. We know that in this area both countries produce both commodities, but which country is exporting cloth and importing corn? To clarify this point, we need to introduce the *no-trade line*; that is, the locus of all points in which the two countries could potentially trade, but each country produces exactly the amounts of corn and cloth required by domestic consumers. Thus alongside the *no-trade line* the value of cloth produced in each country is exactly equal to the rents obtained in that country, so that no trade takes place between the two countries. This is also the line that is crossed by a trajectory when the accumulation of capital pushes one country from a situation in which the country exports cloth to a situation in which the same country exports corn, and *vice versa*. This line is represented in green in Figure 5.3 and therefore it will also be referred to as the green line. It has two different branches: one below the purple line and one above the purple line (see Section 5.A1 for details).

In Figure 5.3, I have also inserted the parts within the *no specialization area* of three possible trajectories (depending on the point in which the world economy is at time zero). They are indicated as segments of straight lines in black. Let us consider segment *AB*. It is part of a trajectory entering the *no specialization area* in point *A*, crossing the green line and then the segment *CD* in point *B*. It is clearly

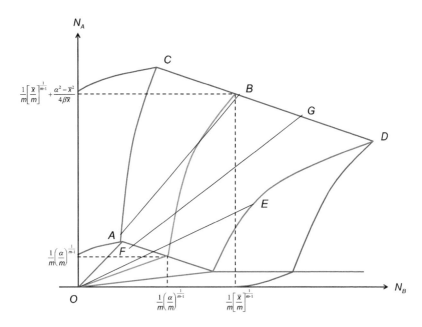

Figure 5.3 The patterns of trade.

a trajectory in which, at the beginning, country *B* is specialized in corn production. Then the accumulation of capital pushes country *B* to produce both commodities, though it is still exporting corn, but once the green line is crossed, country *B* starts to export cloth and import corn. Accordingly, country *B* joins the stationary state as a cloth exporter.

The case of segment *OE is* slightly different. It is part of a trajectory starting in the *no specialization area*, crossing the green line and then leaving the *no specialization area* in point *E*. It is clearly a trajectory in which, at the beginning, country *A* is a cloth exporter; the accumulation of capital then pushes it to become a corn exporter. Finally, country *A* becomes specialized in the production of corn. Further, the trajectory could either enter again the *no specialization area* and arrive at the stationary state in a point internal to segment *CD* or persist in the *A specialized area* until the stationary state is reached in point *D*.

The analysis of segment *FG* may be particularly interesting because the trajectory starts in point *F*. The obvious interpretation is that countries were in a situation of autarky before time 0 and at time 0 they start to trade. Hence in the autarky phase (just before time 0) country *A* is obliged to cultivate land of low quality to feed its own population, whereas at time 0 (in which the economy is open to trade) country *A* becomes a cloth exporter and is accordingly free to leave idle the plots of land of low quality since point *F* is below the purple line. (The process can be delayed by adjustment costs.) Yet the accumulation of capital pushes country *A* not only to cultivate the low-quality land again, but also to become a corn exporter.

5.6 Another example

In the example introduced and discussed in detail in the previous four Sections 5.2–5.5, both countries have plots of land of the best quality. As mentioned above, this excludes the possibility of a country specializing in the production of cloth. This section introduces and briefly discusses an example in which a country can be specialized in cloth production. The example will also show that the accumulation of capital may push one country from being specialized in cloth production to being specialized in corn production.

The example analysed in this section is identical to the previous example except that (i) country *B* has only low-quality land and (ii) the surface area of low-quality land is the same in both countries. The phase space of the example is presented in Figure 5.4 (the equations of the different lines are listed in an appendix, Section 5.A2; the

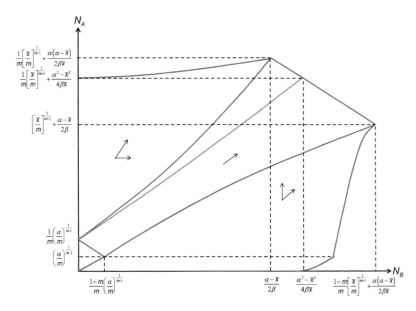

Figure 5.4 The phase space of the second example when $m = 1/2$, $\alpha = 2$, $\beta = 1/2$.

construction of these curves is left to the reader, as an exercise). The area to the left of the purple line is the area in which land of low quality is not cultivated, and therefore, country B is specialized in production of cloth. In this area, both countries share the same rate of profits and therefore also the same rate of growth. It is immediately verified that it is possible to plot a straight line passing through the origin on the left of the purple line that cuts both the green line and the blue line. A segment of this straight line is part of a trajectory in which country B is initially specialized in the production of cloth, then starts to produce corn (crossing the purple line), then starts to export corn (crossing the green line), and then becomes specialized in corn production (crossing the blue line). Note that before joining the stationary state the trajectory can also re-enter the non-specialized area.

5.7 Ricardo on a case of reversal of the pattern of international specialization among trading countries

In Chapter VII of the *Principles*, in dealing with the example we discussed in Section 4.3 Ricardo asserted:

Now suppose England to discover a process for making wine, so that it should become her interest rather to grow it than import it; she would naturally divert a portion of her capital from the foreign trade to the home trade; she would cease to manufacture cloth for exportation, and would grow wine for herself. The money price of these commodities would be regulated accordingly; wine would fall here while cloth continued at its former price, and in Portugal no alteration would take place in the price of either commodity.

(*Works* I, p. 137)

Hence, Ricardo considered the reversal of comparative advantage which may entail the reversal of the patterns of international specialization. Indeed, the above passage introduces the argument I mentioned in Section 4.3 that, with convertible currencies, comparative advantages play their role through movements of gold and consequent variations in the rate of change of currencies. Hence, the process from the reversal of comparative advantages to the reversal of the patterns of international specialization is achieved, in Ricardo's opinion, through importation and exportation of gold. The question to be answered here is whether the reversal of the patterns of international specialization analysed in this chapter needs the analysis of a process involving importation and exportation of gold and therefore changes in prices in monetary terms. Nothing of this type has been considered in this chapter.

In my opinion, an important difference between the reversal of the patterns of international specialization considered by Ricardo and that analysed here is that Ricardo imagined a technical change in the production of wine for which there occurs a sudden reduction in the number of men whose labour is required in order to produce a given quantity of wine which spasmodically inverted comparative advantages: "England finds that she can employ her labour more productively in the manufacture of wine, and *instantly* the trade of barter between the two countries changes" (*Works* I, p. 140, emphasis added). On the contrary, the changes analysed in this chapter are smooth. Countries *A* and *B* first move in the direction of nullifying the mass of commodities imported and exported, i.e. they move in the direction of autarchy, and only after that the patterns of imports and exports are reversed. This, I think, allows us to avoid a transition period that requires the analysis of monetary aspects.

5.8 Concluding remarks

Although the main source of the chapter is a paper published online about three years after the lectures (see Freni, Salvadori, and Signorino,

2019b), the presentation is much more detailed and it is enriched with a second example. The chapter provides a set of possible trajectories of the world economy. The investigated trajectories are straightforward expressions of what is generally called the structural change triggered by economic development: it is the accumulation of capital that leads countries into economic environments that are different, at times very different, from the initial one.

The issue of structural change is discussed in several works of Classical authors. Freni, Salvadori, and Signorino (2019a) analysed this issue in Malthus (1817, 1826), Torrens (1815), and Ricardo (1822, *Works* IV, pp. 201–270), and showed that all these authors were aware that free international trade triggers a process of structural change within the trading countries. Yet Malthus conceptualized development *as if* structural change was a process going on *only* within agricultural and corn-exporting countries. By contrast, Torrens and Ricardo addressed the phenomenon of structural change on the assumption that the latter was a symmetrical process at work *both* in agricultural *and* manufacturing countries. Differences in their policy proposals (Malthus's endorsement versus Torrens's and Ricardo's rejection of food protectionism) are related to differences in their analyses of the international dimension of the processes of structural change stimulated by free corn trade. As regards Ricardo, he argued that with free trade in the long run some of those less fertile plots of British land that initially would be left idle, because of the import of cheap foreign corn, would be put back under tillage (see segment FG in Figure 5.3). Accordingly, in the absence of restrictive Corn Laws, Great Britain would have imported much less foreign corn than British protectionists dreaded. Yet Ricardo did not explore all the analytical consequences deriving from the fact that differences in land fertility do not exist only within a given country but also among the various trading countries. In particular, he did not consider the possibility that Great Britain could even become a corn-exporting country at a later stage of the worldwide process of capital accumulation and population growth.

5.A1 Appendix: the construction of the phase space

Let us first construct the purple line. As mentioned above, along this line $\bar{x}(1+r_A) = mN_{A1}^{m-1}$ and this value equals ap_2 if cloth is produced in country A; otherwise, it may be larger than ap_2. Three cases must be distinguished. In the first case, *both* countries produce cloth, and therefore,

$$\bar{x}(1+r_A)=\bar{x}(1+r_B)=mN_{A1}^{m-1}=mN_{B1}^{m-1}=ap_2$$

$$R_A=R_B=N_{A1}^m-mN_{A1}^{m-1}N_{A1}=(1-m)N_{A1}^m=(1-m)\left(\frac{\alpha}{m}\right)^{\frac{m}{m-1}}$$

Since the amount of cloth produced in both countries must equal the rents paid in both countries,

$$2(1-m)N_{A1}^m=ap_2\left(N_{A2}+N_{B2}\right)=mN_{A1}^{m-1}\left(N_{A2}+N_{B2}\right)$$

and therefore,

$$\frac{2}{m}N_{A1}=N_A+N_B$$

This is enough to determine the purple line in this case (both inequalities hold if and only if $N_B \geq N_{B1}$ and $N_A \geq N_{A1}$):

$$N_A=\frac{2}{m}\left(\frac{\alpha}{m}\right)^{\frac{1}{m-1}}-N_B$$

$$\left(\frac{\alpha}{m}\right)^{\frac{1}{m-1}}\leq N_B\leq\frac{2-m}{m}\left(\frac{\alpha}{m}\right)^{\frac{1}{m-1}}$$

In the second case, cloth is produced *only* in country *B*. This is enough to determine the purple line in this case:

$$N_A=N_{A1}=\left(\frac{\alpha}{m}\right)^{\frac{1}{m-1}}$$

$$N_B\geq\frac{2-m}{m}\left(\frac{\alpha}{m}\right)^{\frac{1}{m-1}}$$

In the third case, cloth is produced *only* in country *A*, and therefore,

$$\bar{x}(1+r_A)=mN_{A1}^{m-1}=\alpha=ap_2\leq mN_B^{m-1}$$

$$R_A+R_B=(1-m)\left(N_{A1}^m+N_B^m\right)=(1-m)\left[\left(\frac{\alpha}{m}\right)^{\frac{m}{m-1}}+N_B^m\right]$$

$$=ap_2N_{A2}=\alpha\left[N_A-\left(\frac{\alpha}{m}\right)^{\frac{1}{m-1}}\right]$$

This is enough to determine the purple line in this case:

$$N_A = \frac{1}{\alpha}\left[\left(\frac{\alpha}{m}\right)^{\frac{m}{m-1}} + (1-m)N_B^m\right]$$

$$N_B \le \left(\frac{\alpha}{m}\right)^{\frac{1}{m-1}}$$

Let us now determine the brown line. As mentioned above, along this line the rate of profits in at least one country equals zero and therefore $\bar{x} = ap_2$, and this value is not lower than the marginal productivity of labour in the corn production and is equal to it in any country in which cloth is produced. Four parts must be distinguished. In the first part, the rate of profits in both countries equals zero:

$$\bar{x} = mN_{A1h}^{m-1} = \alpha - 2\beta N_{A1l} = mN_{B1}^{m-1} = ap_2$$

and therefore,

$$N_{B1} = N_{A1h} = \left[\frac{\bar{x}}{m}\right]^{\frac{1}{m-1}}$$

$$N_{A1l} = \frac{\alpha - \bar{x}}{2\beta}$$

$$R_A + R_B = 2(1-m)N_{A1h}^m + \beta N_{A1l}^2 = ap_2\left(N_{A2} + N_{B2}\right)$$

from which we obtain

$$2(1-m)\left[\frac{\bar{x}}{m}\right]^{\frac{m}{m-1}} + \beta\left[\frac{\alpha - \bar{x}}{2\beta}\right]^2$$

$$= \bar{x}\left(N_A - \left[\frac{\bar{x}}{m}\right]^{\frac{1}{m-1}} - \frac{\alpha - \bar{x}}{2\beta} + N_B - \left[\frac{\bar{x}}{m}\right]^{\frac{1}{m-1}}\right)$$

This is enough to determine the brown line in this case (both inequalities hold if and only if $N_B \ge N_{B1}$ and $N_A \ge N_{A1}$):

$$N_A = \frac{2}{m}\left[\frac{\bar{x}}{m}\right]^{\frac{1}{m-1}} + \frac{\alpha^2 - \bar{x}^2}{4\beta\bar{x}} - N_B$$

$$\left[\frac{\bar{x}}{m}\right]^{\frac{1}{m-1}} \leq N_B \leq \frac{2-m}{m}\left[\frac{\bar{x}}{m}\right]^{\frac{1}{m-1}} + \frac{(\alpha - \bar{x})^2}{4\beta\bar{x}}$$

In the second part, the rate of profits of country A equals zero, whereas the rate of profits of country B is positive, and therefore $N_{B1} = N_B$:

$$\bar{x} = mN_{A1h}^{m-1} = \alpha - 2\beta N_{A1l} = ap_2 \leq mN_B^{m-1}$$

hence,

$$N_{A1h} = \left[\frac{\bar{x}}{m}\right]^{\frac{1}{m-1}}$$

$$N_{A1l} = \frac{\alpha - \bar{x}}{2\beta}$$

$$R_A + R_B = (1-m)N_{A1h}^m + \beta\left[\frac{\alpha - \bar{x}}{2\beta}\right]^2 + (1-m)N_B^m = ap_2 N_{A2}$$

from which we obtain

$$(1-m)\left[\frac{\bar{x}}{m}\right]^{\frac{m}{m-1}} + \frac{(\alpha - \bar{x})^2}{4\beta} + (1-m)N_B^m = \bar{x}\left(N_A - \left[\frac{\bar{x}}{m}\right]^{\frac{1}{m-1}} - \frac{\alpha - \bar{x}}{2\beta}\right)$$

This is enough to determine the brown line in this case:

$$N_A = \frac{1}{m}\left[\frac{\bar{x}}{m}\right]^{\frac{1}{m-1}} + \frac{\alpha^2 - \bar{x}^2}{4\beta\bar{x}} + \frac{1-m}{\bar{x}}N_B^m$$

$$N_B < \left[\frac{\bar{x}}{m}\right]^{\frac{1}{m-1}}$$

In the third and fourth parts, the rate of profits of country B equals zero, whereas the rate of profits of country A is positive, and therefore $N_{A1} = N_A$. The third part is above the purple line. The fourth part is below the purple line. If low-quality land is cultivated (which obtains in the third part), then

$$\bar{x} = mN_{B1}^{m-1} = ap_2 \leq mN_{A1h}^{m-1} = \alpha - 2\beta N_{A1l}$$

hence,

$$N_{B1} = \left[\frac{\bar{x}}{m} \right]^{\frac{1}{m-1}}$$

$$N_{A1l} = \frac{\alpha - mN_{A1h}^{m-1}}{2\beta} = N_A - g(N_A)$$

$$N_{A1h} = g(N_A)$$

$$R_A + R_B = (1-m)N_{A1h}^m + \beta N_{A1l}^2 + (1-m)N_{B1}^m = ap_2 N_B$$

from which we obtain

$$(1-m)\left[\frac{\bar{x}}{m} \right]^{\frac{m}{m-1}} + \beta \left[N_A - g(N_A) \right]^2 + (1-m)\left[g(N_A) \right]^m$$

$$= \bar{x}\left(N_B - \left[\frac{\bar{x}}{m} \right]^{\frac{1}{m-1}} \right)$$

This is enough to determine this part of the brown line:

$$N_B = \frac{1}{m}\left[\frac{\bar{x}}{m} \right]^{\frac{1}{m-1}} + \frac{\beta}{\bar{x}}\left[N_A - g(N_A) \right]^2 + \frac{1-m}{\bar{x}}\left[g(N_A) \right]^m \qquad (2)$$

$$\left(\frac{\alpha}{m} \right)^{\frac{1}{m-1}} \leq N_A \leq \left[\frac{\bar{x}}{m} \right]^{\frac{1}{m-1}} + \frac{\alpha - \bar{x}}{2\beta}$$

I refrain from writing N_A as an explicit function of N_B. It is enough to remark that the function is well defined since the RHS of equation (2) is increasing.

Let us calculate the fourth part of the brown line. If low-quality land is not cultivated, then

$$\bar{x} = mN_{B1}^{m-1} = ap_2 \leq mN_A^{m-1}$$

hence,

$$N_{B1} = \left[\frac{\bar{x}}{m} \right]^{\frac{1}{m-1}}$$

$$R_A + R_B = (1-m)N_A^m + (1-m)N_{B1}^m = ap_2 N_{B2}$$

from which we obtain

$$(1-m)\left[\frac{\bar{x}}{m}\right]^{\frac{m}{m-1}} + (1-m)N_A^m = \bar{x}\left(N_B - \left[\frac{\bar{x}}{m}\right]^{\frac{1}{m-1}}\right)$$

This is enough to determine this part of the brown line (both inequalities hold if and only if $0 \le N_A \le (\bar{x}/m)^{\frac{1}{m-1}}$):

$$N_A = \left[\frac{\bar{x}}{1-m}N_B - \frac{1}{1-m}\left[\frac{\bar{x}}{m}\right]^{\frac{m}{m-1}}\right]^{\frac{1}{m}}$$

$$\frac{1}{m}\left[\frac{\bar{x}}{m}\right]^{\frac{1}{m-1}} \le N_B \le \frac{2-m}{m}\left[\frac{\bar{x}}{m}\right]^{\frac{1}{m-1}}$$

Let us now determine the red line. As mentioned above, along this line both countries share the same rate of profits, but only country B produces cloth. We have to distinguish two parts: above and below the purple line. In the first part, low-quality land is not cultivated:

$$\bar{x}(1+r_A) = \bar{x}(1+r_B) = mN_A^{m-1} = mN_{B1}^{m-1} = ap_2$$

$$R_A + R_B = 2(1-m)N_A^m = ap_2 N_{B2} = ap_2(N_B - N_A)$$

from which we obtain this part of the red line:

$$N_A = \frac{m}{2-m}N_B$$

$$N_B \le \frac{2-m}{m}\left(\frac{\alpha}{m}\right)^{\frac{1}{m-1}}$$

If the low-quality land is cultivated:

$$\bar{x}(1+r_A) = \bar{x}(1+r_B) = mN_{A1h}^{m-1} = \alpha - 2\beta N_{A1l} = mN_{B1}^{m-1} = ap.$$

hence,

$$N_{A1h} = N_{B1} = g(N_A)$$

$$N_{A1l} = N_A - g(N_A)$$

$$R_A + R_B = 2(1-m)\left[g(N_A)\right]^m + \beta\left[N_A - g(N_A)\right]^2$$
$$= ap_2 N_{B2} = m\left[g(N_A)\right]^{m-1}\left[N_B - g(N_A)\right]$$

from which we obtain

$$(2-m)\left[g(N_A)\right]^m + \beta\left[N_A - g(N_A)\right]^2 = m\left[g(N_A)\right]^{m-1} N_B$$

This is enough to determine this part of the red line:

$$N_B = \frac{2-m}{m} g(N_A) + \frac{\beta\left[N_A - g(N_A)\right]^2}{m\left[g(N_A)\right]^{m-1}} \tag{3}$$

$$\left[\frac{\bar{x}}{m}\right]^{\frac{1}{m-1}} \le N_A \le \frac{2-m}{m}\left[\frac{\bar{x}}{m}\right]^{\frac{1}{m-1}} + \frac{(\alpha - \bar{x})^2}{4\beta\bar{x}}$$

Once more I refrain from writing N_A as an explicit function of N_B. It is enough to remark that the function is well defined since the RHS of equation (3) is increasing.

Let us now determine the blue line. As mentioned above, along this line both countries share the same rate of profits, but only country A produces cloth. We have to distinguish two parts: above and below the purple line. In the first part, low-quality land is not cultivated:

$$\bar{x}(1+r_A) = \bar{x}(1+r_B) = mN_{A1}^{m-1} = mN_B^{m-1} = ap_2$$

$$R_A + R_B = 2(1-m)N_B^m = ap_2 N_{A2} = ap_2(N_A - N_B)$$

from which we obtain this part of the red line:

$$N_A = \frac{2-m}{m} N_B$$

$$N_B \le \left[\frac{\alpha}{m}\right]^{\frac{1}{m-1}}$$

If the low-quality land is cultivated:

$$\bar{x}(1+r_A) = \bar{x}(1+r_B) = mN_{A1h}^{m-1} = \alpha - 2\beta N_{A1l} = mN_B^{m-1} = ap$$

$$R_A + R_B = 2(1-m)N_B^m + \beta\left[\frac{\alpha - mN_B^{m-1}}{2\beta}\right]^2$$

$$= ap_2 N_{A2} = ap_2\left[N_A - N_B - \frac{\alpha - mN_B^{m-1}}{2\beta}\right]$$

from which we obtain

$$(2-m)N_B^m + \frac{\alpha^2 - m^2 N_B^{2(m-1)}}{4\beta} = mN_B^{m-1}N_A$$

This is enough to determine this part of the blue line:

$$N_A = \frac{2-m}{m}N_B + \frac{\alpha^2 N_B^{1-m} - m^2 N_B^{m-1}}{4\beta m}$$

$$\left[\frac{\alpha}{m}\right]^{\frac{1}{m-1}} \leq N_B \leq \left[\frac{\bar{x}}{m}\right]^{\frac{1}{m-1}}$$

Let us now determine the green line. As mentioned above, along this line the cloth produced in each country is exactly equal in value to the rents obtained in that country. We have to distinguish two parts: above and below the purple line. In the first part, low-quality land is not cultivated:

$$\bar{x}(1+r_A) = \bar{x}(1+r_B) = mN_{A1}^{m-1} = mN_{B1}^{m-1} = ap_2$$

$$R_A = (1-m)N_{A1}^m = ap_2 N_{A2} = ap_2(N_A - N_{A1}) = mN_{A1}^{m-1}(N_A - N_{A1})$$

$$R_B = (1-m)N_{B1}^m = ap_2 N_{B2} = ap_2(N_B - N_{B1}) = mN_{B1}^{m-1}(N_B - N_{B1})$$

from which we obtain this part of the green line:

$$N_A = N_B$$

$$N_B \leq \frac{1}{m}\left(\frac{\alpha}{m}\right)^{\frac{1}{m-1}}$$

If the low-quality land is cultivated:

$$\bar{x}(1+r_A) = \bar{x}(1+r_B) = mN_{A1h}^{m-1} = \alpha - 2\beta N_{A1l} = mN_{B1}^{m-1} = ap_2$$

$$R_A = (1-m)N_{A1h}^m + \beta\left[\frac{\alpha - mN_{A1h}^{m-1}}{2\beta}\right]^2$$

$$= ap_2 N_{A2} = mN_{A1h}^{m-1}\left(N_A - N_{A1h} - \frac{\alpha - mN_{A1h}^{m-1}}{2\beta}\right)$$

$$R_B = (1-m)N_{B1}^m = ap_2 N_{B2} = mN_{B1}^{m-1}(N_B - N_{B1})$$

from which we obtain

$$N_{A1h} = N_{B1} = mN_B$$

$$(1-m)(mN_B)^m + \beta\left[\frac{\alpha - m(mN_B)^{m-1}}{2\beta}\right]^2$$

$$= m(mN_B)^{m-1}\left(N_A - (mN_B) - \frac{\alpha - m(mN_B)^{m-1}}{2\beta}\right)$$

This is enough to determine this part of the green line:

$$N_A = N_B + \frac{\alpha^2 m^{-m}N_B^{1-m} - m^m N_B^{m-1}}{4\beta}$$

$$\frac{1}{m}\left(\frac{\alpha}{m}\right)^{\frac{1}{m-1}} \leq N_B \leq \frac{1}{m}\left[\frac{\bar{x}}{m}\right]^{\frac{1}{m-1}}$$

5.A2 Appendix: the details of the second example

The purple line consists of two parts:

$$N_A = \frac{1}{m}\left(\frac{\alpha}{m}\right)^{\frac{1}{m-1}} - N_B, \qquad 0 \leq N_B \leq \frac{1-m}{m}\left(\frac{\alpha}{m}\right)^{\frac{1}{m-1}}$$

$$N_A = \frac{m}{1-m}N_B \qquad\qquad 0 \leq N_B \leq \frac{1-m}{m}\left(\frac{\alpha}{m}\right)^{\frac{1}{m-1}}$$

The brown line consists of four parts:

$$N_A = \frac{1}{m}\left[\frac{\bar{x}}{m}\right]^{\frac{1}{m-1}} + \frac{\alpha^2 - \bar{x}^2}{4\beta\bar{x}} + \frac{\beta}{\bar{x}}N_B^2, \qquad 0 \le N_B \le \frac{\alpha - \bar{x}}{2\beta}$$

$$N_A = \frac{1}{m}\left[\frac{\bar{x}}{m}\right]^{\frac{1}{m-1}} + \frac{\alpha^2 - \bar{x}^2}{2\beta\bar{x}} - N_B,$$

$$\frac{\alpha - \bar{x}}{2\beta} \le N_B \le \frac{1-m}{m}\left[\frac{\bar{x}}{m}\right]^{\frac{1}{m-1}} + \frac{\alpha(\alpha - \bar{x})}{2\beta\bar{x}}$$

$$N_B = \frac{\alpha - \bar{x}}{2\beta}\left[\frac{\alpha - \bar{x}}{2} + \bar{x}\right] + \frac{\beta}{\bar{x}}\left[N_A - g(N_A)\right]^2 + \frac{1-m}{\bar{x}}\left[g(N_A)\right]^m,$$

$$\left(\frac{\alpha}{m}\right)^{\frac{1}{m-1}} \le N_A \le \left[\frac{\bar{x}}{m}\right]^{\frac{1}{m-1}} + \frac{\alpha - \bar{x}}{2\beta}$$

$$N_A = \left[\frac{\bar{x}}{(1-m)}N_B - \frac{\alpha^2 - \bar{x}^2}{4(1-m)\beta}\right]^{\frac{1}{m}},$$

$$\frac{\alpha^2 - \bar{x}^2}{4\beta\bar{x}} \le N_B \le \frac{\alpha^2 - \bar{x}^2}{4\beta\bar{x}} + \frac{1-m}{m}\left(\frac{\alpha}{m}\right)^{\frac{1}{m-1}}$$

The blue line consists of one part:

$$N_A = \frac{1}{m}\left[\frac{\alpha - 2\beta N_B}{m}\right]^{\frac{1}{m-1}} + \frac{2\beta N_B^2}{\alpha - 2\beta N_B} + N_B, \qquad 0 \le N_B \le \frac{\alpha - \bar{x}}{2\beta}$$

The red line consists of two parts, but one coincides with part of the purple line. The other is:

$$N_B = \frac{(1-2m)\left[g(N_A)\right]^m - 2\beta\left[N_A - g(N_A)\right]g(N_A) + \alpha N_A}{\alpha - 2\beta\left[N_A - g(N_A)\right]},$$

$$\left[\frac{\alpha}{m}\right]^{\frac{1}{m-1}} \le N_A \le \left[\frac{\bar{x}}{m}\right]^{\frac{1}{m-1}} + \frac{\alpha - \bar{x}}{2\beta}$$

The green line consists of one part:

$$N_A = \frac{1}{m}\left[\frac{\sqrt{\alpha^2 + 4\beta^2 N_B^2} - 2\beta N_B}{m}\right]^{\frac{1}{m-1}} + \frac{\left[\alpha + 2\beta N_B - \sqrt{\alpha^2 + 4\beta^2 N_B^2}\right]^2}{4\beta\left[\sqrt{\alpha^2 + 4\beta^2 N_B^2} - 2\beta N_B\right]}$$

$$+ \frac{\alpha + 2\beta N_B - \sqrt{\alpha^2 + 4\beta^2 N_B^2}}{2\beta}, \qquad 0 \le N_B \le \frac{\alpha^2 - \bar{x}^2}{4\beta\bar{x}}$$

Note

1 Indeed, as we saw in Chapter 4, a country may be specialized in cloth production if the marginal productivity of labour in the corn sector is lower than ap_2, and this may be the case even if the population employed in the corn production is nought. As a consequence, the rate of profits in such a country coincides with the rate of profits holding in all countries that produce both corn and cloth.

References

Bajona, C. and T.J. Kehoe (2010). Trade, growth and convergence in a dynamic Heckscher-Ohlin model. *Review of Economic Dynamics*, **13**(3): 487–513.

Barro, R.J. and X. Sala-i-Martin (1995). *Economic Growth*. New York: McGraw-Hill.

Bellino, E. (2015). Pasinetti, Luigi Lodovico, on Ricardo, in Heinz D. Kurz and Neri Salvadori (eds). *The Elgar Companion to David Ricardo*. Cheltenham, UK and Northampton, MA: Edward Elgar, pp. 396–404.

Bellino E. and S. Nerozzi (2017). Causality and interdependence in Pasinetti's works and in the modern classical approach. *Cambridge Journal of Economics*, **41**(6): 1653–1684.

Bhaduri, A. and D. Harris (1987). The complex dynamics of the simple Ricardian system. *Quarterly Journal of Economics*, **102**: 893–901.

Burgstaller, A. (1986). Unifying Ricardo's theory of growth and comparative advantage. *Economica*, **53**(212): 467–481.

Chen, Z. (1992). Long-run equilibria in a dynamic Heckscher-Ohlin model. *The Canadian Journal of Economics*, **25**(4): 923–943.

Ciccone, R. and P. Trabucchi (2015). Corn model, in Heinz D. Kurz and Neri Salvadori (eds). *The Elgar Companion to David Ricardo*. Cheltenham, UK and Northampton, MA: Edward Elgar, pp. 92–105.

Costa, G. (1985). Time in Ricardian models: Some observations and some new results, in G. A. Caravale (ed). *The Legacy of Ricardo*. Oxford: Basil Blackwell, pp. 59–83.

D'Alessando, S. and N. Salvadori (2008). Pasinetti *versus* Rebelo: Two different models or just one? *Journal of Economic Behavior & Organization*, **65**(3–4): 547–554.

de Vivo, G. (2015). David Ricardo's *An essay on the effects of a low price of corn on the profits of stock*. *History of Economics Review*, **62**(1): 76–97.

Deleplace, G. (2017). *Ricardo on Money: A Reappraisal*. London: Routledge.

Eatwell, J. 1984 [1995]. Piero Sraffa: Seminal economic theorist. *Science & Society*, **48**(2): 211–216, reprinted in J.C. Wood. *Piero Sraffa, Critical assessment*. London and New York: Routledge, 1995, pp. 74–79.

Fiaschi, D. and R. Signorino (2003). Income distribution and consumption patterns in a 'classical' growth model, in Neri Salvadori (ed). *The Theory of Economic Growth: A 'Classical' Perspective.* Cheltenham, UK and Northampton, MA: Edward Elgar, pp. 81–102.

Fiaschi, D. and R. Signorino (2006). Natural wages dynamics in a Ricardian growth model, in Neri Salvadori and Carlo Panico (eds). *Classical, Neo-Classical and Keynesian Views on Growth and Distribution.* Cheltenham, UK and Northampton, MA: Edward Elgar, pp. 27–53.

Findlay, R. (1974). Relative prices, growth and trade in a simple Ricardian system. *Economica,* **41**(161): 1–13.

Freni, G. (1991). Capitale tecnico nei modelli dinamici ricardiani. *Studi Economici,* **44**: 141–159.

Freni, G. (2018). Back to the sixties: A note on multi-primary-factor linear model with homogeneous capital. *Metroeconomica,* **69**(1): 125–141.

Freni, G. and N. Salvadori (2019). Ricardo on machinery: An analysis of Ricardo's examples. *The European Journal of the History of Economic Thought,* **26**(3): 537–553.

Freni, G., N. Salvadori and R. Signorino (2019a). Back to agriculture? Malthus (1817 and 1826), Torrens (1815) and Ricardo (1822) on international trade and structural change. *History of Political Economy,* **51**(5): 935–955.

Freni, G., N. Salvadori and R. Signorino (2019b). Structural change in a Ricardian world economy: The role of extensive rent. *Structural Change and Economic Dynamics,* 49: 277–282.

Garegnani, P. (1984). Value and distribution in the classical economists and Marx. *Oxford Economic Papers,* **36**: 291–325.

Heckscher, E. (1919). The effect of foreign trade on the distribution of income [in Swedish]. *Ekonomisk Tidskrift,* 497–512. Translated as chapter 13 in *American Economic Association, Readings in the Theory of International Trade.* Philadelphia, PA: Blakiston, 1949, pp. 272–300; a new translation is provided in H. Flam and M.J. Flanders (eds). *Heckscher-Ohlin Trade Theory.* Cambridge, MA: The MIT Press, 1991, pp. 39–69.

Jones, L.E. and R. Manuelli (1990). A convex model of equilibrium growth: Theory and policy implications. *Journal of Political Economy,* **98**(5): 1008–1038.

Kaldor, N. (1955–56). Alternative theories of distribution. *Review of Economic Studies,* **23**: 83–100.

Kaldor, N. (1957). A model of economic growth. *Economic Journal,* **67**: 591–624.

King, R.G. and S. Rebelo (1990). Public policy and economic growth: Developing neoclassical implications. *Journal of Political Economy,* **98**(5): 126–150.

Kurz, H.D. (2017). A plain man's guide to David Ricardo's principle of comparative advantage, in Shigeyoshi Senga, Masatomi Fujimoto, and Taichi Tabuci (eds). *Ricardo and International Trade.* London and New York. Routledge, pp. 9–19.

Kurz, H.D. and N. Salvadori (1992). Morishima on Ricardo: A review article. *Cambridge Journal of Economics*, **16**(2): 227–247.

Kurz, H.D. and N. Salvadori (1995). *Theory of Production: A Long-Period Analysis.* Cambridge: Cambridge University Press.

Kurz, H.D. and N. Salvadori (1998a). Morishima on Ricardo: A rejoinder. *Cambridge Journal of Economics*, **22**: 227–239.

Kurz, H.D. and N. Salvadori (1998b). "Endogenous" growth models and the "Classical" tradition, in *Understanding 'Classical' Economics. Studies in Long-Period Theory.* London: Routledge, pp. 66–89.

Kurz, H.D. and N. Salvadori (1999). Theories of "endogenous" growth in historical perspective, in M.R. Sertel (ed). *Contemporary Economic Issues. Proceedings of the Eleventh World Congress of the International Economic Association, Tunis, vol. 4: 'Economic Behaviour and Design'.* London: Macmillan, pp. 225–261.

Kurz, H.D. and N. Salvadori (2003). Theories of economic growth: Old and new, in Neri Salvadori (ed). *The Theory of Economic Growth. A 'Classical' Perspective.* Cheltenham, UK and Northampton, MA: Edward Elgar, pp. 1–22.

Kurz, H.D. and N. Salvadori (2006). Endogenous growth in a stylized 'classical' model, in George Stathakis and Gianni Vaggi (eds). *Economic Development and Social Change.* London: Routledge, pp. 106–124.

Kurz, H.D. and N. Salvadori (2010). Trade equilibrium amongst growing economies: Some extensions, in John Vint, Stanley Metcalfe, Heinz D. Kurz, Neri Salvadori, and Paul A. Samuelson (eds). *Economic Theory and Economic Thought. Essays in Honour of Ian Steedman.* London: Routledge, pp. 106–114.

Kurz, H.D. and N. Salvadori (2015). The classical theory of rent, in Mauro Baranzini, Claudia Rotondi, and Roberto Scazzieri (eds). *Resources, Production and Structural Dynamics.* Cambridge: Cambridge University Press, pp. 72–94.

Lucas, R.E. (1988). On the mechanics of economic development. *Journal of Monetary Economics*, **22**: 3–42.

Malthus, Thomas Robert (1817). *An Essay on the Principle of Population, or, A View of Its Past and Present Effects on Human Happiness: With an Inquiry into Our Prospects Respecting the Future Removal or Mitigation of the Evils Which It Occasions.* 5th ed. London: John Murray.

Malthus, T.R. (1826). *An Essay on the Principle of Population, or, A View of Its Past and Present Effects on Human Happiness: With an Inquiry into Our Prospects Respecting the Future Removal or Mitigation of the Evils Which It Occasions.* 6th ed. London: John Murray.

Maneschi, A. (1983). Dynamic aspects of Ricardo's international trade theory. *Oxford Economic Papers*, **35**(1): 67–80.

Maneschi, A. (1992). Ricardo's international trade theory: Beyond the comparative cost example. *Cambridge Journal of Economics*, **16**(4): 421–437.

Maneschi, A. (2015). Corn Laws, in Heinz D. Kurz, and Neri Salvadori (eds). *The Elgar Companion to David Ricardo.* Cheltenham, UK and Northampton, MA: Edward Elgar, pp. 85–92.

Marcuzzo, M.C. (ed.) (1986). *Nicholas Kaldor. Ricordi di un Economista.* Bologna: Garzanti.

Marshall, A. (1920). *Principles of Economics.* 1st ed. 1890, 8th ed. 1920. Reprint, reset. London: Macmillan, 1977.

Morishima, M. (1989). *Ricardo's Economics. A general equilibrium theory of distribution and growth.* Cambridge: Cambridge University Press.

Morishima, M. (1996). Morishima on Ricardo: Two replies. *Cambridge Journal of Economics*, **20**(1): 91–109.

Ohlin, B.G. (1933). *Interregional and International Trade.* Cambridge, MA: Harvard University Press.

Pasinetti, L.L. (1960). A mathematical formulation of the Ricardian system. *Review of Economic Studies*, **27**: 78–98.

Picchio, A. (1998). Subsistence, in Heinz D. Kurz and Neri Salvadori (eds). *The Elgar Companion to Classical Economics.* Cheltenham, UK and Northampton, MA: Edward Elgar, vol. II, pp. 428–434.

Rebelo, S. (1991). Long run policy analysis and long run growth. *Journal of Political Economy*, **99**: 500–521.

Ricardo, D. (1951 ssq.). *The Works and Correspondence of David Ricardo*, 11 volumes, edited by P. Sraffa in collaboration with M.H. Dobb. Cambridge: Cambridge University Press. In the text referred to as *Works*, volume number and page number.

Salvadori, N. (2004). Is Ricardian Extensive Rent a Nash Equilibrium? in R. Arena and N. Salvadori (eds). *Money, Credit and the Role of the State: Essays in Honour of Augusto Graziani.* Aldershot: Ashgate, pp. 349–360.

Salvadori, N. and R. Signorino (2015). Defence *versus* Opulence? An appraisal of the Malthus-Ricardo 1815 controversy on the Corn Laws. *History of Political Economy*, **47**(1): 151–184.

Salvadori, N. and R. Signorino (2016). From stationary state to endogenous growth: International trade in the mathematical formulation of the Ricardian system. *Cambridge Journal of Economics*, **40**(3): 895–912, on-line publication 1 April 2015.

Salvadori, N. and R. Signorino (2017a). From endogenous growth to the stationary state: The world economy in the mathematical formulation of the Ricardian system. *The European Journal of the History of Economic Thought*, **24**(3): 507–527, on-line publication 15 July 2016.

Salvadori, N. and R. Signorino (2017b). The Ricardian system: A graphical exposition, in Shigeyoshi Senga, Masatomi Fujimoto, and Taichi Tabuci (eds). *Ricardo and International Trade.* London and New York: Routledge, pp. 70–92.

Samuelson, P.A. (1948). International trade and equalization of factor prices. *Economic Journal*, **58**(230): 163–184.

Samuelson, P.A. (1949). International factor-price equalization once again. *Economic Journal*, **59**(234): 181–197.

Samuelson, P.A. (1959a). A modern treatment of the Ricardian economy: The pricing of goods and of labor and of land services. *The Quarterly Journal of Economics*, **73**(1): 1–35.

Samuelson, P.A. (1959b). A Modern treatment of the Ricardian economy: Capital and interest aspects of the pricing process. *The Quarterly Journal of Economics*, **73**(2): 217–231.

Samuelson, P.A. (1969). The way of an economist, in P.A Samuelson (ed). *International Economic Relations: Proceedings of the Third Congress of the International Economic Association*. London: Macmillan, pp. 1–11.

Samuelson, P.A. (1978). The canonical classical model of political economy. *Journal of Economic Literature*, **16**(4): 1415–1434.

Shiozawa, Y. (2017). The new theory of international values: An overview, in Y. Shiozawa, T. Oka, and T. Tabuchi (eds). *The New Construction of Ricardian Theory of International Values*. Singapore: Springer, pp. 3–73.

Smith, A. (1976). *An Inquiry into the Nature and Causes of the Wealth of Nations*. 1st ed. 1776, Vol. II of *The Glasgow Edition of the Works and Correspondence of Adam Smith*, edited by R. H. Campbell, A. S. Skinner, and W. B. Todd. Oxford: Oxford University Press. In the text quoted as *WN*, book number, chapter number, section number, paragraph number.

Sraffa, P. (1925). Sulle relazioni fra costo e quantità prodotta. *Annali di Economia*, **2**: 277–328.

Sraffa, P. (1951). Introduction, in Ricardo (1951 ssq.). *Works* I, pp. xiii–lxii.

Sraffa, P. (1960). *Production of Commodities by Means of Commodities. Prelude to a Critique of Economic Theory*. Cambridge: Cambridge University Press.

Sraffa, P. (1998). On the relations between cost and quantity produced, in L. L. Pasinetti (ed). *Italian Economic Papers*. Bologna: Il Mulino and Oxford: Oxford University Press, pp. 323–363; translation of Sraffa, P. (1925); reprinted in H. D. Kurz and N. Salvadori (eds). *The Legacy of Piero Sraffa*. Cheltenham, UK: Edward Elgar, 2003.

Steedman, I. (1979a). *Trade amongst Growing Economies*. Cambridge: Cambridge University Press.

Steedman, I. (ed.) (1979b). *Fundamental Issues in Trade Theory*. London: Macmillan.

Stigler, G.J. (1953). Sraffa's Ricardo. *American Economic Review*, **43**, September, 586–599.

Stirati, A. (1998). Wages, in Heinz D. Kurz and Neri Salvadori (eds). *The Elgar Companion to Classical Economics*. Cheltenham, UK and Northampton, MA: Edward Elgar, vol. II, pp. 528−535.

Torrens, R. (1815). *An Essay on the External Corn Trade; Containing an Inquiry into the General Principles of that Important Branch of Traffic: An Examination of the Exceptions to Which These Principles are Liable and a Comparative Statement of the Effects Which Restrictions on Importation and Free Intercourse Are Calculated to Produce upon Subsistence, Agriculture, Commerce, and Revenue*. London: Hatchard.

Young, A.A. (1928). Increasing returns and economic progress. *The Economic Journal*, **38**: 527–542.

Yukizawa, K. (1974). The original meaning and the deformed interpretation of Ricardo's 'theory of comparative costs' (in Japanese). *Shōgaku Ronsan*, **15**(6): 25–51.

Index

Sala-i-Martin, X. 22
Samuelson, P.A. 3, 20, 29, 60–61, 68,
   82–85; *see also* HOS
Say's Law 4, 28, 32, 25, 73
Second World War 3
Shiozawa, Y. xiii, 86
Signorino, R. xii–xiii, 28, 46, 47,
   50, 52–53, 65, 67, 73, 81, 86, 88,
   103. 104
single production 59–60, 62, 64,
   67–73
small open economy 48–66, 67–69,
   70, 73, 85, 88, 91
Smith, A. 1, 20, 23, 39
Solovian growth theory 23
Spain 92
Sraffa, P. 1–3, 12, 29, 31, 34,
   35, 43
stationary state 6, 21, 26, 31, 33,
   36–38, 39, 51, 54, 64, 74–75, 77,
   91–93, 101–102
Steedman, I. xi, xiii, 69, 83, 86
Stigler, G.J. 1
Stirati, A. 16
Stolper, W. 84–85
structural change 104

surplus approach to the theory of
   value and distribution 1
surplus principle 29

Takenaga, S. xiii, 86
technical change xii–xiii, 19, 23, 32,
   39, 50, 103
'technology' 22, 24, 46, 53, 66
technology 6–8, 12–13, 14, 20–21,
   23–25, 29, 32–33, 39, 44, 46, 55, 69,
   84–85, 89–90, 93–95
Torrens, R. 16–17, 104
Trabucchi, P. 28
trajectory/trajectories 97–102

Ulam, S. 60

wage frontier 60, 63, 66
wage rate: ante-factum 7, 29; post-
   factum 7–8, 10, 15, 20, 28, 29
workers' consumption 39–43, 44, 46, 47
world economy 48–49, 64–65, 67–114

Yorkshire 92
Young, A.A. 20
Yukizawa, K. 86